اللغة العربية للمبتدئين

ARABIC
FOR BEGINNERS

International Edition
Revised and Expanded

ARABIC
FOR BEGINNERS

International Edition

Syed Ali

Hippocrene Books, Inc.
New York

Also by the same Author

دعنا نتحدث بالعربيـــة

Let Us Converse in Arabic

Fifth printing, 2006.

Published in arrangement with:
UBS Publishers' Distributors Ltd.
5, Ansari Road, New Delhi – 110 002, India

For information, address:
HIPPOCRENE BOOKS, INC.
171 Madison Avenue
New York, NY 10016

ISBN 0-7818-0841-3

Printed in the United States of America.

INTRODUCTION

The Arabic language has today assumed the status of an international language. With the emergence of sovereign Arab States in Asia and Africa, interest is evinced in this language by people living in the four corners of the world. It is unique that Arabic, though a classical language, is good enough for an age whose scientific and political vocabulary is increasingly expanding. Time has not driven it into oblivion as it has done in the case of many a mighty tongue, nor has it undergone any drastic change during its more than fourteen centuries of existence. On the other hand, it has revitalized itself and become more popular with the passage of time.

As Philip K. Hitti has remarked, "For many centuries in the Middle Ages it (Arabic) was the language of learning and culture and progressive thought throughout the civilized world. Between the ninth and twelfth centuries more works, philosophical, medical, historical, religious, astronomical and geographical were produced through the medium of Arabic than through any other language." The European languages are indebted to Arabic for part of their vocabulary, idiom and diction. The Oxford English Dictionary reveals the fact that a vast number of English words are of Arabic origin. Its alphabet has been adopted by Persian, Pushtu, Urdu, Sindhi, Turkish, Malay and several other oriental languages.

This volume introduces Arabic to those who wish to learn it through the English medium. This book does not pretend to cover all the finer points of this language, nor does it deal with the principles of grammar exhaustively. Most of the lessons have as their heading a grammatical term. The vocabulary lists of these lessons include the words used in the illustrative texts and the model sentences. In these lists, the plural form of nouns is indicated after a dash, the synonyms after a colon and the imperfect verb forms are shown with the past tense forms.

Translation of one language into another always gives rise to certain difficulties emanating from the distinctive thought forms and cultural patterns. Literal translation is often unidiomatic. I have tried to bring the translation of Arabic expressions as close to the originals as possible.

In the second part of this edition I have added selections from modern Arabic prose and poetry by eminent Arab writers of various countries, including those who had migrated to America and represent different schools of thought. This would be of use to university students in the non-Arab world. The student is advised to read Arabic newspapers and journals and listen to Arabic programs broadcast from various regions in order to keep himself abreast of the latest trends in Arabic literature. It is by no means an easy task to attain mastery over Arabic language, but dedication and sustained effort do produce results.

I am thankful to King Faisal Center for Research in Islamic Studies, Riyadh, Baghdad University and Islamic African Center, Khartoum for suggesting certain changes in the book and these have been incorporated in this edition.

وما توفيقـــي إلا بالله عليه توكلت وإليه أنيب

Syed Ali

7, Begum Street, Royapettah,
(Madras) Chennai, India.

CONTENTS المحتويات
Introduction مقدمة

الجزء الأول : القواعد
First Part : Grammar

الجزء الثاني – مختارات من الأدب العربي الحديث

Second Part : Selections from Modern Arabic Literature

قسم النثر

قسم الشعر

LESSON ONE

The Alphabet حروف الهجاء

خ k̲ ح ḥ ج j ث ṯ ت t ب b ا a

ص ṣ ش sh س s ز z ر r ذ d̲ د d

ق q ف f غ g̅ ع ‘a ظ ẓ ط ṭ ض ḍ

ي y و w هـ h ن n م m ل l ك k

Arabic, like Hebrew, Persian and Urdu, is written and read from right to left*. The Arabic alphabet consists of twenty-eight letters. A letter is a conventional mark to express a sound. Most of the letters take different shapes while constituting the first letter of a word, the last letter of a word or while occuring in between. Some letters which are identical in form are distinguished from one another in writing with the aid of the small dots called *diacritical points* نقطة *Nuqta.*

Name of the letter	Arabic Alphabet		Phonetic symbol
alif	ا	الف	a
hamza	ء – أ	همزة	a
ba	ب	بـــاء	b
ta	ت	تـــاء	t̲

* While practicing writing of this alphabet, always write from right to left, i.e. contrary to the habit you have developed while writing English

Name of the letter	Arabic Alphabet		Phonetic symbol
Tā	ث	ثاء	ṯ
jīm	ج	جِيمْ	j
hā	ح	حَاء	ḥ
ḵā	خ	خَاء	ḵ
dāl	د	دَال	d
ḏāl	ذ	ذَال	ḏ
rā	ر	رَاء	r
zā or zay	ز	زَاء	z
sīn	س	سِين	s
shīn	ش	شِين	sh
sād	ص	صَاد	ṣ
ḍād	ض	ضَاد	ḍ
ṭā	ط	طَاء	ṭ
ẓā	ظ	ظَاء	ẓ
ayn	ع	عَيْن	‘a
ḡayn	غ	غَين	ḡ
fā	ف	فَاء	f

Name of the letter	Arabic Alphabet		Phonetic symbol
qāf	ق	قاف	**q**
kāf	ك	كَاف	**k**
lām	ل	لاَم	**l**
mīm	م	مِيم	**m**
nūn	ن	نُون	**n**
hā	هـ	هَاء	**h**
wāw	و	وَاو	**w**
yā	ي	يَاء	**y**

There are some Arabic consonants which have no equivalent in the English alphabet.

The first letter of the Arabic alphabet i.e. ا (alif) is considered a consonant when it carries the Arabic symbol أ (hamza); otherwise it is considered a long vowel. The symbol used to indicate أ (hamza) in this book is "**a**".

Similarly **ḥ** ح, **k̲** خ, **'a** ع, **ḡ** غ, have no equivalents in the English alphabet. Books of foreign origin have explained at length how the pronunciation of these letters is articulated by twisting the tongue in more than one way. But we have avoided this exercise. Instead of using symbols which could be better understood by academicians and experts of the phonetic system, we have used the familiar English letters with dots and strokes attached to them.

There are letters which may be supposed to convey the same sound, but in fact should be distinctly pronounced. Readers are advised to take care to distinctly pronounce each of the letter of the Arabic alphabet from the start with the help of their teachers. For example ط ث ت should be pronounced distinctly, hence the symbols used for these letters in this book are **t**, **t̲**, **ṭ** respectively. Likewise ح **ḥ** and هـ **h**, س **s** and ص **ṣ**, خ **k̲** and ق **q** and ظ **ẓ**, أ **a** and ع **'a** have their distinct pronunciation.

The letter ض (its phonetic symbol in this book is **ḍ**) is peculiar to Arabic language. The Arabs call their language *the language of* ض لُغة الضَّاد presumably because they deny to non-Arabs the ability to pronounce this consonant.

Some letters of the Arabic alphabet look similar in shape but are distinguished from one another by the position of small dots *diacritical points.* For example ب **b**, ت **t**, ث **t̲** have the same shape, but ب has one dot below, ت and ث have two and three dots on the top respectively.

ج **j**, ح **ḥ** and خ **k̲** are differentiated from one another by the position of the dot or the absence of it. Same is the case with د **d** and ذ **d̲**. ر **r** and ز **z**, س **s** and ش **sh**, ص **ṣ** and ض **ḍ**, ط **ṭ** and ظ **ẓ**, and ع **'a** and غ **g̅**. The letters ي **y** is written with two dots below or without dots.

The letter ت **t** when used as a feminine ending of nouns and adjectives is shaped ة. Observe this change at the end of the following nouns and adjectives.

تِلْمِيْذَةٌ *a female student* جَمِيْلَةٌ *beautiful*

The letter هـ **h** is written as ه : ـه (without dots) when suffixed to nouns e.g كِتَابُهُ kitabuhu *his book.*

LESSON TWO

VOWELS الحركات

Diphthong, Nunation, Doubled Consonant

The Arabic language had originally no signs for the short vowels. When the Arabic language was learnt by non-Arabs and when the verses of the Qur'an were read incorrectly these signs came to be used.

Short vowels are usually not indicated in Arabic books, journals or in any written matter unless the correct pronunciation of a word, according to grammatical principles, needs to be precised. A person who knows Arabic grammar can read correctly any Arabic passage without the help of vowel signs forming part of the text, but a beginner very much needs them.

Every consonant in vocalized Arabic text is provided with a vowel sign (sometimes indicated and often omitted in writing). In the Arabic language a vowel is called حركة "haraka" *movement.* And a consonant with a vowel sign is called متحرك "mutaharrik" *moved.* If a consonant is without a vowel sign, it is called ساكن "sakin" *resting.*

There are three short vowels in the Arabic language. Unlike vowels in English, they are indicated by strokes.

1. الفتحة *Fatha* (a) ـَ is a small diagonal stroke above a consonant, it is identical with the vowel **"a"** in the English word "man" e.g. تَ **ta,** جَ **ja,** فَ **fa**.

2. الضمة *Damma* (u) ـُ a small "و" *waw* above a consonant. It is identical with the vowel "**u**" in the English word "bull" e.g. تُ **tu**, جُ **ju,** فُ **fu**.

3. الكسرة *kasra* (i) ـِ a small diagonal stroke under a consonant, it is identical with "**i**" in the English word "finish" e.g. تِ **ti,** جِ **ji,** فِ **fi,** رِ **ri,** لِ **li,** مِ **mi**.

Read each of these consonants, once with *Fatha* ـَ, the second time with *Damma* ـُ and a third time with *Kasra* ـِ.

Long Vowels and Diphthongs

Three of the consonants ا و ي which are described by the grammarians as حُرُوف الْعِلَّة "huruf al illa" *weak* or *irregular letters*, are used for lengthening the vowels.

ا for **a**, ي for **i** and **ai**, و for **u** and **au** . e.g.

رَاء ra, فِي fi, ذُو du, لَوْ lau.

"ا" corresponds to ـَ, "ي" corresponds to ـِ and "و" corresponds to ـُ. Therefore "ا" is called "أُخْتُ الْفَتْحَة" *the sister of fatha*, "ي" "أُخْتُ الْكَسْرَة" *the sister of kasra*, and "و" "أُخْتُ الضَّمَّة" *the sister of damma*. Thus نَهَارُ 'naharu' as opposed to نَهَرَ 'nahara , جُودٌ 'jūdun' as opposed to جَوَدَ 'jawada' and صَدِيقٌ 'sadīqun' as opposed to صَدَقَ 'sadaqa'.

When the weak letters are used as lengtheners they do not admit any vowel sign.

"Fatha" ـَ before "ي" and "و" form the diphthongs **ai** and **au** e.g. رَيْبٌ "raibun" *doubt*, مَوْجٌ "maujun" *wave*.

Here some Arabic words are written, with the component letters shown separately, and with the vowel marks indicated.

Remember that if an Arabic word consists of two, three or more letters, all these are written together except و ز ر ذ د ا which are not joined to the letter that follows them. e.g. برق - جاء - دع (Lesson 3 deals with this subject).

تَ رَ كَ	فَ هِـ مَ	كَ تَ بَ	رَ كِ بَ	وَ صَ لَ
taraka	fahima	kataba	rakiba	wasala
to leave	*to understand*	*to write*	*to ride*	*to connect*
رَ زَ قَ	نَ صَ رَ	ذَ هَـ بَ	لَ عِ بَ	وَ زَ نَ
razaqa	nasara	dahaba	laaiba	wazana
to provide	*to help*	*to go*	*to play*	*to weigh*
ضَ رَ بَ	فَ تَ حَ	سَ كَ نَ	كَ رُ مَ	سَ مِ عَ
daraba	fataha	sakana	karuma	samia
to hit	*to open*	*to dwell*	*to be noble*	*to hear*
شَ رِ بَ	اَ كَ لَ	بَ حَ ثَ	لَ بِ سَ	تَ عِ بَ
shariba	akala	bahata	labisa	taaiba
to drink	*to eat*	*to search*	*to wear*	*to work hard*

Nunation التنويـــن

When nouns and adjectives are indefinite, the vowel signs are written double e.g. بً بٌ بٍ. In such a case the pronunciation of the word changes. Letter ب with one "Fatha" is pronounced as "ba". But the same ب with double "Fatha" is pronounced as "ban". Likewise ت **tan**, ج **jan**, ف **fan**. Letter ب with one 'Damma' is pronounced "bu". But the same ب with double 'Damma' is pronounced as "bun". Thus ت **tun**, ج **jun**, ف **fun**. Letter بِ with one 'Kasra' is pronounced as "bi", but the same letter with double kasra ـٍ is pronounced "bin". Likewise تٍ **tin**, جٍ **jin**, فٍ **fin**.

The sound produced as a result of double vowel signs ـًـٌـٍ on a consonant is called تَنْوِيْن *nunation*, i.e. though ن "**n**" is not written its sound is added to that of the vowel.

Note: A word with the definite article ال will not accept nunation.

In the following, each letter of the alphabet is written with double "Fatha" ـً , double "Damma" ـٌ and double "Kasra" ـٍ , read them aloud.

اً ٌ ٍ بً ٌ ٍ تً ٌ ٍ ثً ٌ ٍ جً ٌ ٍ حً ٌ ٍ خً ٌ ٍ دً ٌ ٍ ذً ٌ ٍ رً ٌ ٍ زً ٌ ٍ سً ٌ ٍ شً ٌ ٍ صً ٌ ٍ

ضً ٌ ٍ طً ٌ ٍ ظً ٌ ٍ عً ٌ ٍ غً ٌ ٍ فً ٌ ٍ قً ٌ ٍ كً ٌ ٍ لً ٌ ٍ مً ٌ ٍ نً ٌ ٍ هـً ٌ ٍ وً ٌ ٍ يً ٌ ٍ

Some examples:

بِ نْ تٌ	اِ بْ نٌ	اُ مٌّ	اَ بٌ	اُ سْ رَ ةٌ
bintun	ibnun	ummun	abun	usratun
daughter	*son*	*mother*	*father*	*family*

زَ وْ جَ ةٌ	زَ وْ جٌ	جَ دٌّ	اُ خْ تٌ	اَ خٌ
zaujatun	zaujun	jaddun	ukhtun	akhun
wife	*husband*	*grandfather*	*sister*	*brother*

Absence of Vowel السُّكُوْن

When a consonant is without any vowel mark it is called سَاكِن "sakin" *resting*, and the sign used to indicate this is ـْ a small circle placed over a quiescent consonant. When one consonant in a word is with the vowel sign and the following letter is سَاكن *sakin*, the two letters would form a syllable, i.e. they would be read together and thus produce a joint sound.

Some examples:

مِ نْ	لَ مْ	هَـلْ	دَ عْ	هَ بْ	خُ ذْ	قُ مْ	كَ مْ
min	lam	hal	da`	hab	k̲ud̲	qum	kam
from	*no*	*is?*	*let*	*give*	*take*	*stand*	*how much*

فِ يْ	لَ ا	مَ ا	لَ وْ	كَ يْ	قُ لْ	كُ نْ	بَ لْ
fī	lā	mā	lau	kai	qul	kun	bal
in	*no*	*what?*	*if*	*so that*	*say*	*be*	*but*

The following words consist of three letters but two syllables. In دَ رْ سٌ "darsun" *lesson* "دَ رْ" are combined and their joint sound is added to the last letter, "س".

نَ فْ سٌ	فَ وْ قَ	حَ مْ دٌ	خَ مْ سٌ	دَ ا رٌ	وَ زْ نٌ
nafsun	fauqa	ḥamdun	k̲amsun	darun	waznun
spirit	*top*	*praise*	*five*	*house*	*weight*

لُ طْ فٌ	كِ ذْ بٌ	خُ بْ زٌ	عِ لْ مٌ	زَ هْ رٌ	جِ سْ رٌ
luṭfun	kid̲bun	k̲ubzun	‘ilmun	zahrun	jisrun
kindness	*lie*	*bread*	*knowledge*	*flower*	*bridge*

Words of two syllables are accented on the first syllable. Three syllable words are accented on the first unless the middle syllable is closed.

Doubled Consonant التَّشْدِيـــدُ

When a consonant occurs twice, one after the other, without a vowel sound in between, it is written once (unlike in English) and the sign ـّـ called شَــدّ *shadda* is placed over it, as رَبٌّ "rabbun" *Lord.*

The consonant on which ـّـ *shadda* is placed has to be distinctly pronounced twice. e.g.

فُكِّرَ	قَصَّ	مَدَّ	ظَنَّ	شَدَّ	شَمَّ
fukkira	qaṣṣa	madda	ẓanna	shadda	shamma
thought over	*to cut*	*to stretch*	*to assume*	*to harden*	*to smell*

A consonant is doubled, and receives *Shadda*, only when a vowel precedes and follows it. The vowel sign is placed over this diacritic sign in case of *"fatha"* or *"damma"*, but is placed underneath if the vowel is "kasra" e.g:

ـَّـ ـُّـ ـِّـ

All consonants can be doubled and take the *"Shadda"* which is also known as *"Tashdid"*.

LESSON THREE

Changing Shapes of the Arabic Alphabet

Those who study Arabic for the first time, meet with the problem of recognizing Arabic letters when they combine to form words. A student who masters the English alphabet can recognize the letters in a word, because the shape of English letters (Roman script) is constant whether they stand alone or form part of a word. But such is not the case with Arabic characters. In manuscript or in print, letters are interwoven with one another and form that may be called ligatures. A letter is written in a slightly different form in a word according to whether it;

1. stands alone, e.g. د ع
2. constitutes the initial letter عـاد
3. is joined to a preceding and following letter فعـل
4. constitutes the final letter in a word سمـع

Note the shape of letter ع in the second, the third and fourth example where it occurs in the beginning, middle and the final positions respectively.

The following chart illustrates the above variations:

Examples (3)	Examples (2)	Examples (1)	(3) Terminal letter	(2) joined to the preceding and following letters	(1) Initial letter	Alone
ماء	باز	أب	با	با	ا	ا
māa	bāz	ab				
water	*hawk*	*father*				

Examples (3)	Examples (2)	Examples (1)	(3) Terminal letter	(2) Joined to the preceding and following letters	(1) Initial Letter	Alone
قلْبٌ	كَبِيرٌ	بَيْتٌ	ـب	ـبـ	بـ	ب
qalb	kabir	bait				
heart	*big*	*house*				
بِنْتٌ	كِتَابٌ	تِيْنٌ	ـت	ـتـ	تـ	ت
bint	kitab	tin				
girl	*book*	*fig*				
حَدِيْثٌ	كَثِيْرٌ	ثَمَرٌ	ـث	ـثـ	ثـ	ث
hadit	katir	tamar				
talk	*abundant*	*fruit*				
مُزْعِجٌ	شُجَاعٌ	جِسْرٌ	ـج	ـجـ	جـ	ج
muz'ij	shuja'a	jisr				
annoying	*brave*	*bridge*				
مِلْحٌ	بَحْرٌ	حِبْرٌ	ـح	ـحـ	حـ	ح
milh	bahr	hibr				
salt	*sea*	*ink*				
شَيْخٌ	نَخْلٌ	خُبْزٌ	ـخ	ـخـ	خـ	خ
shaik̲	nak̲l	k̲ubz				
old man	*date-palm*	*bread*				

جَدِيْدٌ	مَدْرَسَةٌ	دَرْسٌ	ـد	ـد	د	د
jadīd	madrasa	dars				
new	*school*	*lesson*				
مُنْذُ	مَذْهَبٌ	ذَرَّةٌ	ـذ	ـذ	ذ	ذ
mund̲u	mad̲hab	darra				
since	*faith*	*atom*				
وَزِيْرٌ	مِرْوَحَةٌ	رَأسٌ	ـر	ـر	ر	ر
wazīr	mirwaḥa	ras				
minister	*fan*	*head*				
رَمْزٌ	مِيْزَانٌ	زَمِيْلٌ	ـز	ـز	ز	ز
ramz	mīzān	zamīl				
symbol	*scale*	*colleague*				
مِجْلِسٌ	مِسْمَار	سَمَاءٌ	ـس	ـسـ	سـ	س
majlis	mismār	samā				
assembly	*nail*	*sky*				
حَشِيْشٌ	كَشَّافٌ	شَمْسٌ	ـش	ـشـ	شـ	ش
ḥashīsh	kashāf	shams				
grass	*scout*	*sun*				
قَفَصٌ	مِصْبَاحٌ	صَيْفٌ	ـص	ـصـ	صـ	ص
qafaṣ	miṣbāh	ṣaif				
cage	*lamp*	*summer*				
مَرِيْضٌ	فَضْلٌ	ضَامِنٌ	ـض	ـضـ	ضـ	ض
marīḍ	faḍl	ḍāmin				
sick	*favor*	*guarantor*				

Examples (3)	Examples (2)	Examples (1)	(3) Terminal letter	(2) Joined to the preceding and following letters	(1) Initial letter	Alone
غَلَطٌ	مَطَارٌ	طِفْلٌ	ـط	ـطـ	طـ	ط
ḡalaṭ	maṭār	ṭifl				
mistake	*airport*	*child*				
حَفِظَ	مَنْظَرٌ	ظَرْفٌ	ـظ	ـظـ	ظـ	ظ
ḥafiẓa	manẓar	ẓarf				
to keep	*sight*	*envelope*				
بَيْعٌ	طَعَامٌ	عِنَبٌ	ـع	ـعـ	عـ	ع
bai'a	ṭa`ām	'inab				
selling	*food*	*grape*				
بَلِيْغٌ	بَبْغَاءُ	غُلَامٌ	ـغ	ـغـ	غـ	غ
balīḡ	babḡā	ḡulām				
eloquent	*parrot*	*boy*				
شَرِيْفٌ	نَفْعٌ	فَرْدٌ	ـف	ـفـ	فـ	ف
sharīf	naf'a	fard				
noble	*gain*	*individual*				
أُفُقٌ	بَقَرَةٌ	قَلَمٌ	ـق	ـقـ	قـ	ق
ufaq	baqara	qalam				
horizon	*cow*	*pen*				

سَمَكٌ	مَرْكَبٌ	كَشْكُولٌ	ـك	ـكـ	كـ	ك
samak	markab	kashkūl				
fish	*ship*	*notebook*				
قُفْلٌ	جِلْدٌ	لَحْمٌ	ـل	ـلـ	لـ	ل
qufl	jild	laḥm				
lock	*skin*	*mutton*				
شَكْلٌ	مُتَكَلِّمٌ	كُلِّيَّةٌ	ـكل	ـكلـ	كلـ	كل
shakl	mutakallim	kulliya				
figure	*speaker*	*college*				
كَرِيْمٌ	نَمِرٌ	مَطَرٌ	ـم	ـمـ	مـ	م
karīm	namir	maṭar				
generous	*tiger*	*rain*				
وَطَنٌ	مِنْقَارٌ	نَهْرٌ	ـن	ـنـ	نـ	ن
waṭan	minqār	nahr				
country	*beak*	*river*				
وَجْهٌ	مُهَاجِرٌ	هِلَالٌ	ـه	ـهـ	هـ	هـ
wajh	muhājir	hilāl				
face	*emigrant*	*crescent*				
جَوٌّ	قَوْمٌ	وَهْمٌ	ـو	ـو	و	و
jaww	qaum	wahm				
atmosphere	*people*	*suspicion*				
كُرْسِيٌّ	حَيْوَانٌ	يَدٌ	ـي	ـيـ	يـ	ي
kursi	haywān	yad				
chair	*animal*	*hand*				

Broadly speaking, the shape of a letter does not undergo a radical change when in the last position. e.g.

ع in بيْع, ل in قُفـل, ح in مِلْح, ت in بِنْت

But while in the middle position i.e. preceded and followed by other letters, only the initial portion of the letter is used, e.g.

ع "عـ"	ط "ط"	ص "صـ"	س "سـ"
ج "جـ"	هـ "هـ"	م "مـ"	ل "لـ"
ك "كـ"	ق "قـ"	ف "فـ"	ت "تـ"

Minute semicircles are used when ي , ن , ش , س , ث , ت , ب are used in the middle; بَيَّنْتُكَ "bayyantuka" *I made clear to you,* when split would show that it consists of letters ب ي ن ت ك.

These six letters و , ز , ر , ذ , د ,ا cannot be joined to the letters that follow.

Illustrations:

أب ــ درس ــ مذهب ــ رأس ــ زميل ــ وهــم (see chart)

Note: Nouns and adjectives, when indefinite and in the singular number, should be read with double ـٌ ـٍ ـً 'un' (nunation) at the end. For example, the first word in the above chart أبٌ *father* should be read as "abun", likewise other nouns and adjectives.

LESSON FOUR

Definite Article "ال" الشمسية والقمرية
The Sun Letters and The Moon Letters

ال is the definite article of Arabic language, it is the equivalent of the word "the" in English.

Any noun or adjective without ال is considered indefinite. There is no particular sign for the indefinite as "a" in English.

Nouns and adjectives, when indefinite and in the singular number, end with double vowel marks, e.g.

بَيْتٌ	جَمِيْلَـــةٌ	كِتَـــابٌ
house	*beautiful*	*book*

But when these words are made definite by adding ال they end with a single vowel mark only, e.g.

اَلْبَيْتُ	اَلْجَمِيْلَـــةُ	اَلْكِتَـــابُ
the house	*the beautiful*	*the book*

Note: The definite article ال is prefixed to the nouns and adjectives it defines. It does not stand alone. Compare the following words with and without ال

اَلْبَيْتُ : بَيْتٌ اَلْجَمِيْلَةُ : جَمِيْلَةٌ اَلْكِتَـــابُ : كِتَابٌ

The letters of the alphabet are divided into *Sun letters* اَلْحُرُوفُ الشَّمْسِـــيَّةُ "alhuruf-al-shamsiya" and *Moon letters* اَلْحُـــرُوفُ الْقَـــمَرِيَّـــةُ "al huruf-al-qamariya". The "Sun letters" are the dentals ت ث د ذ ر ز س ش ص ض ط ظ ل ن. They are called so because the first letter of the word شَمْسٌ *Sun* is ش which belongs to this category.

When the definite article ال is prefixed to a noun or an adjective beginning with any one of the "Sun letters", the ل being a "Sun letter" itself, is assimilated i.e. ل is not pronounced, though it is written, and the letter next to it is pronounced twice and "*shadda*" ـّـ is written over the initial Sun letter. e.g.

الشَّمْسُ	الرَّجُلُ	النَّصِيْحَةُ	الدِّيْنُ	السَّنَةُ
as-shams	ar-rajul	an-naṣīha	ad-dīn	as-sana
the sun	*the man*	*the advice*	*the religion*	*the year*

The Moon letters are: ا ب ج ح خ ع غ ف ق ك م و هـ ي. They are so called because the word قَمَرٌ *moon,* begins with one of these letters. The definite article ال, when prefixed to any word whose initial letter is a Moon letter, ل is both written and pronounced, e.g.

الْقَمَرُ	الْحَمْدُ	الْفَاكِهَةُ
al-qamar	al-ḥamd	al-fākiha
the moon	*the praise*	*the fruit*

Some Arab grammarians instead of dividing the letters into Sun letters and Moon letters, classify the definite article as ال الشمسية and ال القمرية "the Sun al" and "the Moon al".

The Weak Letters حُرُوفُ الْعِلَّةِ

Three of the consonants ا و ي are named as حُرُوفُ الْعِلَّةِ *al huruf al illa* i.e. "weak" or "irregular" letters. These three letters are often interchanged or dropped under the influence of other letters e.g: قول becomes قال. Consonants other than ا و ي are known as الحُرُوف الصَّحِيحَة *al-huruf as-sahiha* the "sound letters" because under no circumstances they are dropped.

The Shortened "Alif" الألف الـمَقْصُورة

There are some words where ا is indicated not in its full shape but by a short vertical stroke. This is known as الألف الـمَقْصُورة "the shortened alif". However this does not change the pronunciation. e.g.

سَعىٰ ــ ارتَضىٰ ــ الْمُصْطَفىٰ ــ الْمُرْتَضىٰ ــ مُوْسىٰ ــ عِيْسىٰ

The letter ي with which these words end is not pronounced.

The Stretched "Alif" الألف الـمَمْدُودة

In a word when Hamza comes immediately after a vowel-less ألـف the sign آ called "madda" (مَدّ) *stretched* is written on الف. This "alif" is lengthened while pronouncing the word. This is called الألف المَمْدُودة the "stretched" or "extended" alif. e.g.

حَمْرآء	سَوْدآء	بَيْضَآء
red	*black*	*white*

LESSON FIVE

Parts of Speech

Classroom

أجزاء الكلام (الجملة)

حجرة الدراسة

1. The students gather in the classroom to acquire knowledge. The teacher explains the lessons to them and writes (the) important points on the board.

١ - يَجْتمعٌ الطلابُ في حُجْرة الدراسة لِطلب الْعِلْم. المُدرس يَشْرَح الدروس لهُمْ ويكتُب النُّقط المُهمّة علي السَّبُّورة.

2. Each student sits on a chair. In front of him is a table, on it he keeps the books, notebooks and pens.

٢ - وكُلّ طالب يجلس علي الكُرسِي وأمامه منْضدَة يَضَع فوقها الكتب والدفاتر والقلم.

3. On the wall there is a map of the Arab World. It indicates, in different colors, the national boundaries, oil wells and the location of the cities and also agricultural and industrial areas.

٣ - وتُوجد على الْحائِط خريطة العالم العربي التي توضح الحدود القومية وآبار النفط ومواقع المدن وكذلك مناطق الزراعية والصناعية بألوان مختلفة.

4. The teacher writes on the black board (the) questions and (the) exercises. And the students copy them in their notebooks:

٤ - المدرّس يكْتُبُ على السبُّورة السوداء الأسئلة والتمْرينَات والطُّلابُ ينقلُونها في كرّاستِهم.

5. Sometimes discussion on a particular topic takes place; the students participate in it. The teacher points out to them the books wherein information about the topic is found.

٥ - وأحْياناً تَجْري الْمُناقشَة عن موضوع معيَّن يشْترِكُ فِها الطُّلابُ. الأستَاذ يُشيِرُ إليهم الكُتُب التي تُوجدُ فيها معلومات عن الموضوع.

The above sentences are formed by a group of words. A sentence which conveys complete sense is called الجُملة المفيدة. The parts of speech or sentence are called أجزاء الجملة.

Arab grammarians have divided the parts of speech into three categories : (1) إسم *Noun,* (2) فعل *Verb,* (3) حرف *Particle.* But it is such a broad division that adjectives, pronouns, demonstrative pronouns are catalogued as أسماء *Nouns.* Prepositions, interjections and conjunctions are called as حروف *Particles,* أفعال *Verbs* are almost the same as in English.

In paragraph No. 1 الطلاب *the students,* العلم *knowledge,* المدرس *the teacher,* الدروس *the lessons,* النقط المهمة *the important points,* السبُّورة *the board* are broadly grouped under أسماء *Nouns.* In the same paragraph يجتمع *gather,* يشرح *explains,* يكتب *writes* are أفعال *Verbs* ; في *in* ل *for* و *and,* على *on* are حروف *Particles.*

Each part of speech and its different categories are discussed under separate chapters.

VOCABULARY

ḥāit	حائط – حيطان	aswad	أسود
wall		*black*	
k̲arīṭa	خريطة	aṣfar	أصفر
map		*yellow*	
ʻalam al ʻArabi	عالم العربي	azraq	أزرق
Arab world		*blue*	
laun	لون – الوان	bunni	بُنّي
color		*brown*	
sami'a	سمع ؛ يسمع	ak̲ḍar	أخضر
to hear		*green*	

sāmi'a	سامع : مستمع	abyaḍ	أبيض
listener		*white*	
ḥujra	حجرة–حجرات	aḥmar	أحمر
room		*red*	
ḥujra-t- al-dirāsa	حجرة الدراسة	'alā	على : فوق
classroom		*on, above*	
makān	مكان–امكنة	rakiba	ركب ؛ يركب
place		to ride	
ijtamā'a	اجتمع ؛ يجتمع	rākib	راكب
to gather		*rider*	
zara'a	زرع ؛ يزرع	darrāja	دراجة–دراجات
to cultivate		*bicycle*	
fallāh	فلاح–فلاحون	fataḥa	فتح ؛ يفتح
peasant		*to open*	
bi'r	بئر	miftāḥ	مِفتَاح
well		*key*	
karīm	كريم	qufl	قُفل
generous		*lock, bolt*	
waṭan	وطن	bāb	باب–ابواب
country		*door*	
qalam	قلم–اقلام	qaṣab assukkar	قصب السكر
pen		*sugarcane*	
tāus	طاؤوس	shajar	شجر–اشجار
peacock		*tree*	

azīm عظيم
great

ustād استاذ : معلم
teacher

ṭālib طالب – طلاب
student

sharaḥa شرح ؛ يشرح
to explain

dars درس – دروس
lesson

madrasa مدرسة–مدارس
school

kataba كَتب ؛ يكتُب
to write

kātib كاتِبٌ
writer

kitāb كِتَاب – كتُبُ
book

sabbūra سَبُّورة
blackboard

ṭabāshīr طبَاشِير
chalk

jamīl جمِيل
beautiful

maṭar مطر
rain

samā سماء – سماوات
sky

bint بنت – بنات
girl

dahaba ذهب ؛ يذهب
to go

dāhib ذاهِب
one who goes

ṣana'a صنع ؛ يصنع
to manufacture

ṣāni' صانِع
manufacturer

maṣna مصْنَع
factory

ṣinā'a صِناعَة
industry

qaumi قومِي – قومِيات
national, ethnic, racial

'arabi عربِي
Arab

ḥadd حد – حدود
border, edge

jalasa جلسَ ؛ يجْلِس

to sit

jālis جَالِس

one who sits

kursi كُرسِي

chair

minḍada مِنضدَة

table

maktab isti'lāmāt مكتَب الإستعلامات

information office

ḥiḏā حِذَاء – احذِيَة

shoe, sandal

jild جِلْد

leather

shab شَعب

people

mauqa مَوْقع–موَاقِع

location

zirā'a زراعَة

agriculture

suāl سُوال – اسئِلة

question

jawāb جَواب – اجوِبَة

answer

nazala نَزل ؛ ينزلُ

to descend

jama'a جمعَ ؛ يجْمَعُ

to collect, gather

zahr زهْر – ازْهَار

flower

maidān مَيدَان

open place, field

daula دولـــة – دول

country

ḏakara ذكَر ؛ يذْكُر

to remember

istiḏkār استِذْكار

memorizing

muṭābiq مُطَابِق

in agreement with

karrāsa كَرَّاسة : كشكُول

notebook

ṭarīqa طريقـــة – طُرُق

way, method

muallaq مُعلَّق

hanging

ashāra اشارَ ؛ يُشِير

to point out

tamrīn	تمْرين – تمارين	sāir : kull	سائـــر : كُل
exercise		*all*	
mada	مَدَى	mādda	مـــادّة – موَاد
range		*material, subject*	
qudra	قُدْرة : استِعدَاد	mauḍū	مَوضُوع
power, capacity		*topic, theme*	
fahima	فهِمَ ؛ يفْهَمُ	ḥaḍara	حضَرَ ؛ يحْضُرُ
to understand		*to be present*	
'āṣima	عَاصِمَة – عَواصِم	ḥāḍir	حَاضِر
capital city		*present, attending*	
malūmāt	معْلُومات	muḥāḍara	مُحاضَرة
information, data		*lecture*	
marūf	معْرُوف	'arafa	عَرفَ ؛ يعْرف
well-known, fairness		*to know*	

The following Arabic sentences further exemplify the grammatical principle that forms the subject matter of this lesson.

TRANSLATION	***MODEL SENTENCES***
1. The Arabs are generous.	١– الشّعب العربي كريـــم
2. Rain falls from the sky.	٢– ينزل المطرُ من السَّماء
3. Mahmood rode (on) the bicycle.	٣– ركِب محمود الدَّرَّاجــة
4. The green color is beautiful.	٤– اللّون الأخْضرُ جميلٌ
5. The peasant cultivates sugarcane.	٥– يزرَع الفلاّحُ قصبَ السُّكر
6. The peacock is on the tree.	٦– الطاؤوسُ فوق الشجَر
7. Sami went to the school.	٧– ذهبَ سَامِي الى المدْرَسة

LESSON SIX

Adjective and Noun Qualified

الصِّفَــة والمَوصُوف (النَّــعْتُ)

1. The wise man is advising.	١- الرَّجُل العَاقِلُ نَاصِح
2. The big house is comfortable.	٢- البَيتُ الكَبِيرُ مُرِيح
3. The intelligent boy is successful.	٣- الوَلَدُ الذَّكِيُّ نَاجِح
4. The red rose is fine.	٤- الوَرْد الأحْمرُ طَيِّب
5. The ripe date is sweet.	٥- التَّمرُ النَّاضِجُ حُلْوٌ
6. The severe cold is painful.	٦- البَرْد الشَّدِيدُ مُؤْلم
7. The sincere teachers are present.	٧- المُعلِّمُون المُخْلِصُون حَاضِرون
8. The beautiful girl is sitting.	٨- البِنْتُ الجَمِيلَة جَالِسَة
9. Good land is costly.	٩- الأرضُ الجيِّدَة غَالِيَــة
10. The clean gardens are numerous.	١٠- الحَدَائِقُ النَّظِيفَةُ كَثِيْرَة
11. The Arabic language is of a high standard.	١١- اللُّغَةُ العربِيَّةُ رَاقِيَةٌ

The adjective in Arabic is called الصِّفَــة. It is one variety of a noun. المُرَكَّب التَّوصِفِي or "*adjectival construction*" consists of a noun qualified and an adjective. The sentences in this lesson consist of a subject and a predicate. The subject itself consists of two words, the "*noun qualified*" and the "*adjective*". The first word is a noun; it is also called مَوصُوف – مَنْعُــوت "*that which is qualified*", the second word is صِفَــة *adjective*, also called نَعْت.

The adjective has to agree with the noun in respect of gender, number and definite and indefinite form, and in respect of case ending. The noun in sentence No.1. الرَّجـل *the man*, is masculine, singular and definite; so is its adjective العَاقِـل *the wise.* When the same adjective عاقل is to be used for a female, it would be said المَرأة العَاقِلَـة نَـاصِحة *the wise woman is advising.*

All the eleven sentences in this lesson start with الموصـوف or المنعُـوت *the noun qualified* immediately followed by الصِّفة or النعت *adjective* or *description.* The above rule is followed in all but sentence No. 10, in the phrase الحدائق النَّظيفة *the clean gardens.* In this sentence, the adjective does not agree with the noun in respect of number; الحدائِـق is the plural of الحديقـة *the garden.* When the noun qualified is an object, and is plural, masculine or feminine, its adjective would mostly be singular and in the feminine gender. e.g.

البُيُـوت الكبيْـرة	*The big houses*

However when such nouns are in the dual number, their adjectives should agree with the noun. e.g.

الحُجرَتَان الكَبيرتَان مُقفلَتَان	*The two big rooms are locked.*
الشَّجرَتَان الكَبيرتَان مُثمِرتَان	*The two big trees are fruitful.*

Note: In the Arabic language the noun qualified comes before the adjective. e.g.

الـولَـدُ الذَّكِـيٌّ	*the intelligent boy*
البِنْتُ الـجميلـة	*the beautiful girl*

VOCABULARY

‘aāqil	عـــاقِل – عُقلاء
wise	
bait	بَيت – بُيُوت
house	
murīh	مُريح
comfortable	
d̲aki	ذكِيٌّ
intelligent	
ṭayyib	طيِّب
good, pleasant	
ḥulw	حُلو
sweet, charming	
ḥāmid	حامِض
sour, acid	
murr	مُـــرّ
bitter, severe	
muk̲lis	مُخْلِص
sincere	
jayyid	جيِّـــد
excellent	
ḥadīqa	حَدِيقـــة – حدَائِق
garden	

rajul	رجُل-رجَال
man	
imra’a	إمرأة : نساء
woman	
naṣaḥa	نصحَ ؛ ينْصَح
to advise	
nāṣiḥ	ناصِح – نصحاء
adviser	
naṣīḥa	نصِيحة – نصائِح
advice	
kabīr	كبير – كِبار
big	
walad	ولـــد – اولاد
boy	
najaḥa	نجح ؛ ينْجَح
to be successful	
nājiḥ	نَـــاجِح
successful	
warda	وَرْدَة
rose	
tamar	تَمَر
dried date	

katir كَثِير
many, much

raqiya راقِيَـــة
developed, sublime

shadid شدِيـــد
severe

nazara نظرَ ؛ ينْظُر
to see

nazir نَـــاظِر
spectator, director

manzar مَنْظر-منَاظِر
sight

ard أرْض-أراضِي
earth

allugat al ‘arabia اللُّغة العربية
Arabic language

alam ألم
pain, ache

mulim مُؤلِم
painful, distressing

talaba طلب ؛ يطْلُب
to seek

talab طلب
application, demand

nadaja نَضَج ؛ ينضَج
to be ripe

nadij نَاضِج
ripe

faras فَرَس-افْرَاس
horse

ahabba احَبَّ ؛ يُحِبُّ
to love, like

mahbub مَحبُوب
lovable

‘ilm عِلْم-علوم
knowledge, science

galiya غَالِيَـــة
costly

nazif نَظِيْف
clean

wasak وسخ
dirty

nafa’a نفعَ ؛ ينْفَع
to be useful

nafi’a نَـــافِع
useful

tamar ثمر-أثمار
fruit

maṭlūb مطلُوب
desired, wanted

muqaddim at-ṭalab مُقدِّم الطلب
applicant

'inda aṭ-ṭalab عِند الطلب
on demand

ta'aiba تعِبَ ؛ يتْعَب
to work hard

mut'ib مُتعِب
tiresome, dull

ṭawīl طويــل
long

akala اكلَ ؛ يأكُــل
to eat

akaltu أكلتُ
I ate

ihdinā إهْدِنــا
lead us

ṣirāt صِراط
way

mustaqīm مُستقِيم
straight

yaum يوم – ايَــام
day

muṯmir مُثْمِرة
fruitful

'aarūs عرُوس : عريس
bridegroom

'aarūsa عرُوسة
bride

ṣadīq صدِيق
friend

ḥarb حرْب
war

ṣifr صِفْر
zero, nothing

ju ' جــوع
hunger

jāi' جــائِــع
hungry

istiqlāl إستِقْلال : حُرِّيَّــة
independence, freedom

jara جرَى ؛ يجْري
to flow, take place

ijrā' إجراء – إجراءات
enforcements, steps

ijrāt qānūuniya إجراءات قانونية
legal proceedings

nahr نهــر – أنهار
river

hāmm, muhimm هام : مُهم
important, significant

ihtimām إهتِمام
care, attention

t̠aub ثــوب – ثِيَــاب
dress

ḡazīr غزيــر
abundant, heavy

kat̠īf كَثِيف
thick

samīn سَمِين
fat

nahīl نَحِيــل
thin, slim

saḥāb, ḡaim سحاب : غيم
cloud

jadīd جدِيــد
new

'atīq عَتِيــق
old, ancient

mustadīra مُستدِيــرة
round

qaratu قرَاتُ
I read

labisa لبِس ؛ يلْبَس
to wear

malabis ملابِس
clothes

shariba شَرب ؛ يشْرَب
to drink

shārib شَــارب
drinker

sakrān سَكْران
intoxicant, a drunk

t̠awr ثور – ثِيران
bull

ḥarat̠a حرث ؛ يحْرُث
to plough

ḥārit̠ حــارث – حُرّاث
ploughman

qaṭafa قطفَ ؛ يقْطِف
to pick, to pluck

ḥawla حــول
around

sayyāra سيَّــارَة – سيَّارات
car

nādir	نــادِر	nasiya	نَسِيَ : يَنسى
unusual, precious		*to forget*	
ishtaraitu	اشْتَرَيتُ	sara'a	سَرَع ؛ يَسْرَع
I purchased		*to be quick*	
baṭi'	بَطِيء	sarī	سَرِيــع
slow, lazy		*fast*	

The following Arabic sentences exemplify the grammatical principle that has been explained in this lesson.

TRANSLATION	*MODEL SENTENCES*
1. Useful knowledge is desired.	١ - العِلم النَّافِع مَطلُوب
2. The fruit-bearing tree is useful.	٢ - الشَّجرَة المُثمِرة نافِعة
3. The long journey is tiresome.	٣ - السفرُ الطويل مُتْعِب
4. The appearance of the bride is beautiful.	٤ - مِنظرُ العروسة رائع
5. Faithful friends are rare.	٥ - الأصدِقاء الأوفياء نادر
6. I ate sweet apple.	٦ - أكلتُ تفاحــةً حُلوة
7. Lead us to the straight path.	٧ - اهدِنا الصراط المُستقِــم
8. A hungry cat meows.	٨ - يمُوء قِطّ جائــع
9. The assiduous student succeeds.	٩ - ينجَح التّلميذ المُجتهد
10. Independence day is a great day.	١٠ - يومُ الإستِقلال يوم عظيــم
11. In India there are flowing rivers.	١١ - فــي الهنــد أنهار جاريــة
12. Spring is a beautiful season.	١٢ - الرَّبيــع فصل جميــل
13. Wear a clean dress.	١٣ - الْبَسْ ثوبــا نَظِيفــا
14. I drank cold water.	١٤ - شربتُ ماء بــاردا

15. Abundant rain fell.	١٥- نـــزل مطـــر غزيـــر
16. Thick clouds are in the sky.	١٦- السّحاب الكثِيف في السمـــاء
17. The two fat bulls are ploughing.	١٧- الثوران السمِينان يحْرُثان
18. The new book is in the library.	١٨- الكِتابُ الجدِيد في المكتَبَة
19. I picked a red rose.	١٩- قطفتُ وردة حمراء
20. We sat at a round table.	٢٠- جلسنـــا حول مائِدة مستدِيرة
21. This is a fast car.	٢١- هـــذه سيـــارة سريعـــة
22. I purchased a precious watch.	٢٢- اشترَيتُ ساعة نادرة
23. This is a black cap.	٢٣- هـــذه قلنســـوة سوداء
24. I read an important announcement.	٢٤- قرأتُ اعـــلانا هـــاما

LESSON SEVEN

Gender المُذكَّر والمؤنَّث

With regard to gender, Arabic nouns are divided into two categories: (1) مُذكر *masculine* and (2) مؤنث *feminine*. It is essential to know the gender of all nouns as the verbs and adjectives have to agree in respect of the gender of their subjects and the nouns qualified.

(a) Agreement of the verb with its subject:

Hamid wrote.	كتب حـــامـــد
Fathima wrote.	كتبتْ فـــاطمـــة

Whereas for حـــامد the verb used is كتَبَ, for فاطمـــة the verb used is كتَبَـــتْ; though the verb is same, in the first example it is masculine and in the second it is feminine.

(b) Agreement of the adjective with the noun qualified (See lesson Six)

The intelligent boy	الولـــد الـــذَّكيُّ
The intelligent girl	البنتُ الذَّكيَّـــة

Note the "ـــة" (ت) at the end of the feminine adjective.

Feminines are of two kinds.

(1) المؤنث الحقيقـــي *the natural or real feminines*. These are nouns denoting female persons. e.g.

إمـــرأة	أخْت	أمٌّ
woman	*sister*	*mother*

(2) مؤنث غير حقيقـــي *unreal or supposed feminines*. e.g.

أرضُ	شَمْسُ	مدينة
earth	*sun*	*city*

Masculine nouns do not require any sign to signify their gender, but the feminine nouns and adjectives usually end in three specific ways.

(a) Feminines mostly end with "ة" or "ـة".

جميلــة نِعمــة قُـدرة ظلمة

beautiful *blessing* *power* *darkness*

خليفـــة *caliph* and علاّمة *very learned* are exceptions. Though they end with "ة" they are masculine.

(b) Feminines ending with الألف الـممدودة *the shortened alif*

بيضـــآء ســوداء صحراء كِبرياء

fair lady *black* *desert* *pride*

Here is a list of nouns which are feminine but without any specific feminine ending.

(a) Parts of the body which are in pairs but حاجب *eyebrow* is masculine.

أذن ثـدي كتف يـــد كـف فـخذ

ear *breast* *shoulder* *hand* *palm* *thigh*

ســاق رجـل قـدم ســن إصبــع عيــن

shank *leg* *foot* *tooth* *finger* *eye*

(b) Some natural objects which are feminine by mere usage:

نفس أرض نـــار ريــح شمس عين

soul *earth* *fire* *wind* *sun* *fountain*

(c) Names of countries, cities and tribes are feminine:

هنــــد دمشــق قــريش

India *Damascus* *Quraish*

LESSON EIGHT

Singular, Dual and Plural المفرد والمثنى والجمع

A peculiar feature of the Arabic language is that its nouns, adjectives and verbs have three numbers. In this respect it is akin to sanskrit.

1. Singular مفرد – واحد (2) Dual تثنية (3) Plural جمع

As has been explained earlier, the adjectives of the noun qualified (lesson six) and the predicate of the subject (See lesson nine) should agree in respect of number. e.g.

A sincere servant came جاء خادم مخلص (Singular مفرد)

Two sincere servants came جاء خادمان مخلصان (Dual تثنية)

Many sincere servants came جاء خدام مخلصون (Plural جمع)

Agreement of the predicate with the Subject in respect of number: e.g.

The carpenter is working النجار عامل (Singular مفرد)

Two carpenters are working النجاران عاملان (Dual تثنية)

Many carpenters are working النجارون عاملون (Plural جمع)

The dual is formed by adding ان to the singular in the Nominative case and by adding ين in the Accusative and Genitive cases. A word in the dual number does not admit التنوين *nunation*

Singular		**Dual**		
house	بيت	بيتان	or	بيتين
door	باب	بابان	or	بابين
city	مدينة	مدينتان	or	مدينتين

There are two kinds of plurals in Arabic, الجمعُ السَّالم *the sound plural* and جمع التكسير *the broken plural.* When a plural retains all the vowels and consonants of the singular and is based on the standard pattern, it is known as الجمعُ السَّالم as opposed to جمع التكسير.

In most authoritative Arabic dictionaries, the plural of all nouns is given along with the meaning.

Some examples of جمـعُ المذكـر السَّـالم *The Sound Plural Masculine.*

	Plural			**Singular**
writer	كاتبين	or	كاتبون	كاتب
believer	مُؤمِنين	or	مُؤمِنُون	مؤمن
learned	عالِمين	or	عالِمُون	عالم
Egyptian	مِصْرِيين	or	مصريون	مِصريٌّ

Some examples of جمع التكسير *The Broken Plural*

man	رجال	رجل	food	أطعِمة	طعام
blue	زُرق	أزرق	youth	فِتيان	فتى
black	سُود	أسود	red	حُمُر	أحمر
guest	أضياف	ضَيف	ass	حمير	حِمار
hero	أبطال	بطل	earth	أراضي	أرض
loaf	أرغفة	رغيف	group	فِرَق	فِرقة

The plural of مـرأة *woman* is نِساء *women.* Besides the nouns and adjectives, verbs and pronouns too are converted into dual and plural numbers.

LESSON NINE

The Nominal Sentence — الجُملة الإسميَّة
Subject and Predicate — الـــمُبْتَدأ والْخَبْرُ

1. Knowledge is light.	١- العِلمُ نـــورٌ
2. The two teachers are present.	٢- المُعلّمانِ حاضِرَان
3. The engineers are experts.	٣- المُهنْدِسُون ماهِرُون
4. The students are industrious.	٤- الطُّلاّب مُجْتَهِدُون
5. Fathima is intelligent.	٥- فاطِمَـــةُ ذَكِيَّـــة
6. The two girls are writing.	٦- البِنتَـــانِ كاتِبَتَـــان
7. The mothers are kind.	٧- الأمَّهَـــات رَحِيمَـــات
8. The schools are open.	٨- المَدارِسُ مَفْتُـــوحَـــة

All these Arabic sentences consist of two nouns, but in the English translation, invariably the auxiliary verbs "is" and "are" are used to complete the predicate. Though the verbs are not written, the sentence presupposes the presence of a verb. Therefore the first word of each of the above sentences is called مُبتَـــدأ *Subject,* and the second word خَبْرٌ *Predicate.*

Each of the above sentences is called الجُملَة الإسْمِيَّة *the nominal sentence,* because it starts with إســـم *a noun.*

1. Both the subject and the predicate in each of the above sentences are in the Nominative case مرفُـــوع. They end with ـُــ which is the sign of the nominative.

2. Generally المُبْتَـدَأ *the subject* would be definite and الخَبَر *the predicate* indefinite. Note the difference in the meaning of the following:

1. The book is new.	الكِتَـاب جـديد
2. The new book.	الكِتَـابُ الْجدِيـدُ
3. A new book.	كِتَـابٌ جَدِيـدٌ
4. This is a new book.	هـذَا كِـتَـابٌ جَـدِيـدٌ

3. The predicate has to agree with its subject in respect of number and gender.

4. When the subject is the plural form of an object, not a person, the predicate is singular feminine. (see sentence No.8)

5. Particles belonging to groups of كَـانَ and إنّ bring about certain vowel changes in respect of مُبتَدَأ *subject* and خبـر *predicate*. These changes are dealt with in lesson twenty and twenty-one.

Note: The subjects in sentences Nos. 1, 2, 3 and 4 are masculine and in singular, dual and plural respectively. Accordingly there is agreement between the subject and the predicate.

The subjects in sentences Nos. 5, 6, and 7 are feminine and in singular, dual and plural respectively. In all these sentences the predicates are feminine and in accordance with their subjects.

In sentence No. 8 the subject مـدارس *schools* (which is an object, not a person) is in the plural, therefore its predicate مفْتُوحَـة *open* is a feminine singular, The same rule applies to phrases which consist of موصوف *noun qualified* and صِفة *adjective* (see lesson six).

In the following table the agreement of الخبـر *the predicate* with المبتـدأ *the subject* in respect of gender and number is clarified further.

Masculine : مذكَّــر

مُفْــرد	- Singular	– The man is virtuous.	الرجل صالح
تثْنِيَــة	- Dual	- The two men are virtuous.	الرجلان صالحان
جــمع	- Plural	- Many men are virtuous.	الرجال صالحــون

Feminine : مــؤنث

مُفْــرد	- Singular	– The woman is virtuous.	المرأة صالحَة
تثْنِيَــة	- Dual	- The two women are virtuous.	المرأتان صالحتان
جــمع	- Plural	- Many women are virtuous.	النساء صالحــات

Inanimate object : غير عــاقل

مُفْــرد	- Singular	– The star is shining.	الكوكب لامــع
تثْنِيَــة	- Dual	- The two stars are shining.	الكوكبــان لامعان
جــمع	- Plural	- Many stars are shining.	الكواكب لامعــة

VOCABULARY

sulṭān	سلطان : ملك	nūr	نــور
authority, monarch		*light*	
‘aadala	عــدل ؛ يعدِل	muhandis	مُهنْدِس
to act justly		*engineer*	
‘aādil	عــادِل	handasa	هندَسَــة
just person		*engineering*	
tijāra	تِجَــارة	la’aiba	لعِبَ ؛ يلعَب
trade		*to play*	
tājir	تــاجِــر	lā’ib	لاعِــب
merchant		*player*	

amīn أميـــن
trustworthy

ṭibb طِــبّ
medicine

ṭabīb طِبيب
physician, doctor

shams شمْس
sun

qamar قمَـــر
moon

ḍau ضَـــوء
light

muḍi مُضِيء
luminous

ṭala'a طلـــع ؛ يطْلُع
to rise

ṭāli'a طــالِع
rising, ascending

ṭifl طِفــل – أطْفــال
child

nāma نــامَ ؛ ينَـــام
to sleep

naum نـــوم
sleep

umm أم : والِـــدة
mother

ab أب : والِـــد
father

raḥīm رحِيـــم
merciful, kind

ṣalaḥa صَلحَ
to be good

ṣāliḥ صـَــالِح
good, virtuous

kaukab كـــوكِب – كواكِب
star

lāmi'a لامِـــع : براق
shining

ḡurfa غُرفَـــة : حجرة
room

ḡurfa at-tijāra غُرفِة التِّجارة
chamber of commerce

gurfa al-naum غُرفَـــة النـــوم
bedroom

aṯāt أثـــاث
furniture

jaww جـــو
atmosphere, air

ḍaḥika ضَحِكَ ؛ يضْحَك

to laugh

basama بسمَ ؛ يبْسِم

to smile

bāsim بَاسِم : مُبْتَسِم

smiling

laila ليلـــة

night

qaṣura قصُـــر

to be short

qaṣīr, ḍayyiq قصِير : ضيِّق

short, small

wāsi'a وَاســـع

spacious

ḍarra ضَـــرَّ ؛ يضُر

to harm, hurt

ḍarar ضَرَر : خسارة

loss, damage

ḡāba غَاب ؛ يغِيب

to disappear

ḡāib غَـــائِب

absent

d̲ahab ذهَبٌ

gold

laṭīf لطِيف

gentle

aljins al-laṭeef الجِنْس اللّطِيف

the fair sex

miqyās alḥarāra مِقْياسُ الحَرَارة

thermometer

jundi جُندِي

soldier

tashjī'a تِشْجِيع

encouragement

shujā'a شُجَـــاع

courageous

musta'idd مُستَعِـــد

prepared, ready

qadira قَـــدر ؛ يقْـــدِر

to be able

qādir قَـــادِر

able

k̲aṭaba خَطبَ ؛ يْخطُب

to lecture

k̲aṭīb خَطِيب

orator, lecturer

waraq ورق – وراق

paper

madin مَعْدِن

metal, mine

ḥadīd حديـد

iron

nuḥās نُحَـاس

copper

fiḍḍa فِضَّـة

silver

rafa'a رَفَـع ؛ يرْفِع

to raise

rafī'a رفيع : مُرتَفِع : عَـال

high

shāria` شـارع – شـوارع

road

madīna مَدِينَـة – مدُن

city

'amara عَمَـر

to be inhabited, prosper

'aāmir عَـامِر

populous, flourishing

jāhada جَاهد ؛ يُجاهِدُ

to struggle

ijtahada اجتهد ؛ يجْتَهد

to endeavor

nāim نـاعِـم

soft, fine

ni'ma نِعمَـة – نِعم

blessing, favour

nāḍir ناضِر : طازج

fresh, radiant

ṭa'ima طعِمَ ؛ يطْعَم

to taste, eat

ṭa'ām طعـام

food, meal

maṭ'am مَطْعَم

restaurant

ḵāli خـال : فـارغ

vacant, empty

mamlū' مَمْلوء

filled up, loaded

mazaḥa مزَحَ ؛ يمْزَح

to joke

'amila عَمِلَ ؛ يعْمَل

to do, act

qalam arraṣāṣ قلم الرّصاص

pencil

qalam ḥibr jāf قلم حِبر جَاف

ball point pen

The model sentences given below further exemplify the grammatical principle discussed in this lesson.

	TRANSLATION	*MODEL SENTENCES*
1.	The room is narrow.	١- الغُرفَة ضَيِّقَة
2.	The furniture is new.	٢- الأثاثُ جديد
3.	The earth is spacious.	٣- الأرض واسعة
4.	The water is cold.	٤- الماءُ بارد
5.	The weather is pleasant.	٥- الجوّ لطِيتف
6.	The heat is severe.	٦- الحرَارة شديدة
7.	The monarch is just.	٧- السلطان عادِل
8.	The merchant is trustworthy.	٨- التاجِرُ أمِين
9.	The physician is an expert.	٩- الطَّبِيب مَاهِر
10.	The sun is rising.	١٠- الشّمس طالِعَة
11.	The moon is luminous.	١١- القمَر مُضِيء
12.	The stars are shining.	١٢- الكَواكِب لامِعَة
13.	The child is sleeping.	١٣- الطِّفل نَائِم
14.	The mountains are high.	١٤- الجِبَال عالِيَة
15.	The girl is smiling.	١٥- البِنتُ باسِمَة
16.	Time is flying by.	١٦- الوقتُ سريع
17.	The day is long.	١٧- اليوم طويل
18.	The night is short.	١٨- اللّيلة قصِيرَة
19.	The soldier is brave.	١٩- الجُندِيُّ شُجاع
20.	God is powerful.	٢٠- اللهُ قادِر

21. The apple is sweet.	٢١- التُّفاحة حُلوَة
22. The sermon is eloquent.	٢٢- الخُطبَة بَليغة
23. The rain is abundant.	٢٣- المطَرُ غَزير
24. The paper is smooth.	٢٤- الورَق نَاعِم
25. The flowers are fresh.	٢٥- الأزهَار نَاضِرة
26. Iron is useful.	٢٦- الحدِيد نَافِع
27. The food is ready.	٢٧- الطّعام حَاضِر
28. The room is vacant.	٢٨- الغُرفة خَالِية
29. The tank is full.	٢٩- الحَوض مَملوء
30. Much joking is harmful.	٣٠- المَزاح الكَثِير مُضِر
31. The trade is profitable.	٣١- التِّجارة رابِحة
32. The boys are active.	٣٢- الأولاد نشاط
33. The workers are absent.	٣٣- العُمَّال غَائِبُون
34. The female teachers are present.	٣٤- المُعَلِّمات حَاضِرات
35. Gold is a metal.	٣٥- الذَّهبُ معدِن
36. The sky is high.	٣٦- السَّماء مُرتَفِعة
37. The road is narrow.	٣٧- الشّارع ضيِّق
38. The city is crowded.	٣٨- المَدينة عَامِرَة
39. The duck is fat.	٣٩- البطّة سَمِينة
40. The two girls are hardworking.	٤٠- البِنتَان مُجْتَهِدَتَان

LESSON TEN

The Possessive — المُضَافُ والمُضاف إلَيه

1. The Creator of the universe is one. — ١ – خَالِق العَالمِ واحِد
2. God's earth is spacious. — ٢ – أرضُ الله واسِعة
3. The people of India are good. — ٣ – أهلُ الهند طَيِّبون
4. The hospitality of the Arabs is famous. — ٤ – جُود العرب مَشهُور
5. The hands of the boy are clean. — ٥ – يدَا الولَدِ نَظِيفتَان
6. The students of the secondary school are playing. — ٦ – طُلاَّب المدْرَسَة الثَّانوية لاعِبُون
7. Fear of God is the summit of wisdom. — ٧ – رَأس الحِكمَة مَخافة اللهِ
8. Al Azhar University is the center of many sciences. — ٨ – جَامِعة الأزْهَر مَركَز العُلوم المُخْتَلِفة

In the English language the idea of "possession" or "ownership" is conveyed by using apostrophe and s ('s) or the preposition "of". But the same idea is conveyed in Arabic by إضَافة *the construct phrase,* i.e. one noun immediately follows another in such a manner that the second limits or defines the first and renders it definite (without the definite article though).

The first sentence in this lesson خالق العالم واحد *The creator of the universe is one* is a nominal sentence as it begins with a noun خالق. العالم is composed of two words; the definite article ال and عالم *(universe).* The word عالم is in the genitive case because it limits خالق. Thus خالق in this sentence is مضاف and العالم is مضاف إليه .

Note: 1. Both مُضاف and مُضاف إليـــه are nouns.

2. مُضاف would be indefinite and مُضاف إليـــه would either be a proper or a common noun.

3. مُضاف will not accept the definite article ال and "nunation"

4. Due to إضافة the مُضاف إليه ends in ـِ i.e. the genitive case

5. The dual loses its final ن due to إضافة. This change may be noticed in sentence No. 5 where ن is dropped from يدَان.

There are other forms in Arabic which convey the idea of "possession". Besides the use of the possessive pronouns كِتابُهُ *his book* كِتَـابُكَ *your book* كِتَـابِي *my book* (see lesson No. 12) the following words are generally used: ذُو *possessor, owner,* صَاحِب *companion,* أهــل *people.* e.g.

Literally: The possessor of learning *(Learned)* ذُو العِلم

Literally: The companion of learning *(Learned man)* صَاحِب العلم

Literally: The people of learning *(Learned people)* أهل العلم

VOCABULARY

adab أدب
literature, decency

muhaḏḏab مُهَذَّب
polite, courteous

mu'addab مُؤَدب
well-mannered

muṯaqqaf مُثقّف
cultured, educated

adīb أديب
literary man

ṯaqāfa ثقـــافة : حضارة
culture, civilization

asās أساس

foundation, basis

laban, ḥalīb لبن : حليب

milk

baqara بقرة

cow

balad بلد-بلـــدان

country

baladia بلـــدِية

municipality

ḡarb : maḡhrib غرب : مغرب

west

sharq : mashriq شرق : مشرق

east

shimāl شِمال

north

junūb جُنوب

south

ḵidma خِدمـــة

service

istiḵdām استِخدام

to employ

ḵādim خـــادِم

servant

ʻaālam عـــالم : الدنيـــا

universe, world

Allah الله

God

wāḥid واحِـــد

one

ahl: usra أهل : أسرة

family, people

jūd, karam جُود : كرم

generosity

sahīr شهِير : مشهُور

famous

ibtidāia مدرسة ابتدئِيـــة

elementary school

ṯānawia مدرسة ثانويـــة

secondary school

kullia كُلّيـــة

college, faculty

jāmia جـــامِعة

university

m'ahad معهـــد

institute

maktaba مكتبة

library

mutaqaddim مُتقدِّم
advanced, ahead

wazīr وزير - وزراء
minister

wizāra وزارة
ministry

bustān بُستان : حدِيقة
garden

ḥaẓẓ حظ
good luck, fate

d̲ū ḥaẓẓ ذُو حظ
fortunate person

min ḥusn al-ḥaẓẓ من حسن الحظ
luckily, fortunately

ma'a al-asaf مع الأسف
unfortunately

ḡāba غـــابة
jungle

ahrām أهرام
pyramids

'ajal عجــل
haste

'ajala عجلــة
wheel, bicycle

k̲alaqa خلــق
to create

k̲āliq خــالِق
creator

mak̲lūq مخلُوق
creations, created being

k̲auf خَوف : مخافة
fear

k̲āfa خَاف ؛ يخَاف
to fear

raīs رئِيس
chief, president

ḥikma حِكمة
wisdom

ḥakīm حكيم : عـــاقل
wise

rīsha ريشة - ريش
feather

k̲urtūm خُرطوم
trunk

fīl فيــل
elephant

matḥaf متحف - متحفة
museum

kasara كسر ؛ يكسِر

to break

maksūr مكسور

broken

fara' فـرع : غصن

branch, section

ikrām إكرام

respect, honor

dāim دائـم

permanent

muwaqqat مُوقت

temporary

insān إنسان

man

insānia إنسانية

humanity

safar سفر : رحلة

journey, travel

safīr سفِيـر

ambassador

musāfir مُسافِر

traveler

sifāra سِفـارة

embassy

wajaba وجَبَ ؛ يجِب

to be necessary

wājib واجِب

essential, obligatory

wajbat at-ṭa'ām وجبة الطعام

meal, menu

faraḍa فرض

to suppose, to impose

farīḍa فريضـة

duty

matḥaf متحف-متحفة

museum

ḍaif ضيف

guest

muḍīf مُضيف

host

muḍīfa مُضيفة

hostess, stewardess

sharrafa شرَّف ؛ يُشَرِّف

to honor

sharīf شريف

noble

mushrif مُشْرِف

superintendent

The following sentences further exemplify the grammatical principle discussed in this lesson:

	TRANSLATION	*MODEL SENTENCES*
1.	The color of the sky is blue.	١- لـــونُ السماء أزرقُ
2.	The feather of the peacock is excellent.	٢- ريش الطاؤوس جيد
3.	The trunk of the elephant is long.	٣- خُرطوم الفِيل طويـــل
4.	The bay of Bengal is beautiful.	٤- خليج بنغـــال جمِيـــلٌ
5.	Character is the foundation of success.	٥- الأدبُ أساس النَّجاح
6.	Cow's milk is sweet.	٦- لبن البقرَة حُلـــو
7.	The Western countries are advanced.	٧- بُلدان الغربِ مُتقدِّمـــة
8.	The Rector of Al-Azhar University visited India in 1975.	٨- مُدير جامِعَـــة الأزهـــر زَار الهنـــد فـــي سنـــة ١٩٧٥
9.	The doors of the museum are open.	٩- أبواب المتحف مفتُوحـــة
10.	The students of the Cairo University are intelligent.	١٠- تلامِيذ جامعة القاهرة أذكِيـــاء
11.	The lion is the king of the jungle.	١١- الأسد ملك الغـــابـــة
12.	The pyramids of Egypt are ancient.	١٢- أهرام مصر عتيقـــة
13.	The eyes of the cat are bright.	١٣- عينـــا القِطِّ لامِعتان
14.	The (two) wheels of the bicycle are broken.	١٤- عجلتـــا الدراجة مكسورتان
15.	Respect of the guests is essential.	١٥- إكرام الضُّيُوف واجِب
16.	The branch of the tree is green.	١٦- غُصن الشجرةِ أخضرُ
17.	Acquiring knowledge is obligatory.	١٧- طلب العلـــم فريضـــة
18.	School teachers are traveling.	١٨- مُعلِّمو المدرسة مسافرون

LESSON ELEVEN

Personal Pronouns الضمائر المنفصلة

We Work نَحْنُ نعمَل

1. The teacher said to his son: “I work in the school and you study in the college”.

١- قال الأسْتَاذُ لإبْنِــهِ: أنَا اعْمَلُ فِــي الْمدْرَسَةِ وَانْتَ تَتَعَـلَّمُ فِــي الْكُلِّيَّــةِ

2. The girl told her sister: “I work in the post office and you are a doctor in the hospital”.

٢- قالَتْ البِنْتُ لأخْتِهَــا:انَا عَامِلَةٌ فِــي مَكْتَبِ الْبَرِيْــــد وَانْــتِ طَبِيْبَــةٌ فِــي الْمُسْتَشْفَـــى

3. The mother stays at home. She cooks food, brings up the children and looks after the domestic chores.

٣- الأمُّ تَمْكُثُ فِيْ الْبَيْتِ، هِــيَ تَطْبَــخُ الطَّعَــامَ وَتربِّــى وَتَتَــولَّـــى علَــى شُئُونِ الْعَــائِلَــةِ

4. The boy said to his parents: “You have much exerted yourselves and now you will relax.”

٤- قالَ الْوَالِــدُ لِوَالِــدَيْــهِ "تَعِبْتمَــا كَثِيْرا وانْتُمَــا الآنَ تَسْتَرِيْحَانِ وَنَحْــنُ نَخْدِمُكُمَــا"

5. The Director of the establishment told the workers: “Every one of you has made an effort and played his role for achieving the industrial and trade targets of the company, hence you deserve extra allowance”.

٥- قالَ مُدِيْرُ الْمُؤسَّسَةِ للْعُمَّــال: "كُــلُّ وَاحِــدِ مِنْكُمْ بَــذَلَ جُــهْدَهُ وَأدَّى دَوْرَهُ لِتَحْقِيْقِ اهْدافِ الشَّرْكَــةِ الصِّنَــاعِيَّــةِ والتِّجَارِيَّــةِ وَإذاً تَسْتَحِقُّوْنَ عَــلاوَةً

1. Personal pronouns in Arabic are of two varieties:

1) الضَّمَائِر الْمُنْفَصِلَة *unattached* "those which are separate words" e.g. أنَا *I* أنْتَ *you* and نَحْنُ *we*. الضَّمَائِر الْمُنْفَصِلَة are used when the pronoun is in the nominative case.

2) الضَّمَائِر المُتَّصِلَة *attached* "those which are suffixed"

(a) to nouns	(ي)	كِتَابِي	*my book*
(b) to verbs	(ـهُ)	كَتَبْتُهُ	*I wrote it*
(c) to prepositions	(كَ)	لَكَ	*for you*

These suffixes which are attached to a noun, correspond to possessive pronouns of the English language, e.g. كِتَابُهُ *his book.* When they are suffixed to verbs and prepositions, they correspond to personal pronouns in the objective case.

List of الضَّمَائِر المُنْفَصِلَة **Personal Pronouns**

3rd Person Masculine			*Examples*	
1. Singular	he / it	هُوَ	He is a man	هُوَ رجُلٌ
2. Dual	they two	هُمَا	They (two) are men	هُمَا رَجُلاَنِ
3. Plural	they	هُمْ	They are men	هُمْ رِجَالٌ
3rd Person Feminine				
4. Singular	she	هِيَ	She is a woman	هِيَ إمْرَأةٌ
5. Dual	they two	هُمَا	They (two) are women	هُمَا إمْرَأتَانِ
6. Plural	they	هُنَّ	They are women	هُنَّ نِسْوَةٌ

2nd Person Masculine			*Examples*	
7. Singular	You	أَنْتَ	You are a boy.	أَنْتَ وَلَــدٌ
8. Dual	You (two)	أَنْتُمَـــا	You (two) are boys.	أَنْتُمَا وَلَدَانِ
9. Plural	You (all)	أَنْتُمْ	You are boys.	أَنْتُمْ أَوْلاَدٌ
2nd Person Feminine				
10. Singular	You	أَنْتِ	You are a girl.	أَنْتِ بِنْتٌ
11. Dual	You (two)	أَنْتُمَا	You (two) are girls.	أَنْتُمَا بِنْتَانِ
12. Plural	You (all)	أَنْتُنَّ	You are girls.	أَنْتُـــنَّ بَنَـــاتٌ
1st Person Masculine & Feminine				
13. Singular	I (m & f)	أَنَـــا	I am a boy.	أَنَـــا ولَــدٌ
14. Plural	We (m & f)	نَحْـــنُ	We are boys.	نَحْنُ أولاَدٌ
			We are girls.	نَحْـــنُ بَنَـــاتٌ

VOCABULARY

as-sayyid	السيـــد	sabaqa	سبــقَ
Mr.		*to precede, outstrip*	
as-sayyida	السيدة	sābiq	سابق : متقـــدم
Mrs.		*winner, ahead*	
sayyid	سيد – سادة	nashiṭa	نشِط
master, lord		*to be lively*	
sayyida	سيدة – سيدات	nashīṭ	نشيط
lady		*energetic, active*	

aānisa آنسة : فتاة

Miss

ḡani غنـــي - أغنياء

rich

faqīr فقيــر - فقراء

poor

ṣaḥīfa صحيفة : أخبار

newspaper

ṣaḥāfi صحـــافي

journalist

za'īm زعيم : رئيس

leader, chief

za'āma زعامة

leadership

dafa'a دفع ؛ يدفع

to repel, push back

difā'a دفـــاع

defense

k̲aṣib خصب

fertile

mutadil معتدل

moderate, proportionate

shā'ir شاعر

poet

nashāṭ نشاط

activity, briskness

jaish جيش - جيوش

troops

qawi قــوي - أقوى

strong

'alam علــم : رايــة

flag

shakl شكل : صورة

figure

mustaṭīl مستطيل

oblong

dāira دائرة - دوائــر

circle, department

kashafa كشف ؛ يكشف

to uncover

kāshif كاشف : مخترع

discoverer, inventor

al-kashshāfa الكشافة

the scout

ṣannafa صنف ؛ يصنف

to compose, classify

muṣannif مصنف : كاتب

writer

shai’r شعر

poetry

ṣafw صفو

clear, pure

maṣfa مصفى

refinery

‘ā’ila عائلة : عائلي

family, domestic

sha’n شأن – شئون

affair, matter

mā shā’nuka ما شأنك

What do you want?

istirāḥa استراحة

relaxation, rest

mustarīḥ مستريح

relaxing, pleased

tasāmuḥ تسامح

tolerance, leniency

ismaḥ li اسمح لي

permit me, excuse me

k̲aira خيرة – خيرات

good things

murabba مربع

square

naṯr نثـــر

prose

tamṯīlia تمثيلية

drama

mumaṯṯil ممثل

actor, representative

qārra قـــارة

continent

Asia آسيا

Asia

mamlaka مملكة

kingdom

jumhūriya جمهورية

republic

jamhūr جمهور

multitude, people

baḏala بذل ؛ يبذل

to offer, grant

juhd جهد – جهود

effort

baḏl-al-juhūd بذل الجهود

to make efforts

ṭahāra طهارة : تطهير

cleanliness, purification

muṯallaṯ مثلث

triangle, threefold

waṣṭ وسط : متوسط

middle, medium

ḥayawān حيوان

animal

uḵt أخت – أخوات

sister

aḵ اخ – اخوة

brother

ḥayāh حياة : عيش

life

maut موت

death

daur دور – أدوار

role, part

adā أداء : تأدية

rendering of service

ṣadāqa صداقة

friendship

ṣadīq صديق – اصدقاء

friend

'aduw عدو – أعداء

enemy

intiẓār إنتظار

waiting, expectation

jīl جيل – أجيال

generation, people

insān انسان

human being

insāniya انسانية

mankind, politeness

amn, salam امن : سلام

peace, security

al-amn-al-'ālami الأمن العالمي

world peace

al-amn-al-'ām الأمن العام

public safety

rijāl-al-amn رجال الأمن : شرطة

police

maslaḥa مسلحة – مصالح

welfare, government agency

qala' قلعة

fort, stronghold

ḵaima خيمة

tent

'ilawa علاوة

extra allowance, addition

al istishrāq الإستشراق : مستشرق
oriental studies, orientalist

makata مكث ؛ يمكث
to remain, reside

tarbiya تربية
education, upbringing

hadaf هدف - أهداف
target, aim, goal

taḥqīq تحقيق
realization, achievement

mustaḥiq مستحق
deserving, worthy

'uluw علو
height, sublimity

'amaliya عملية
job, making, operation

mu'āmala معاملة
behavior, conduct

ta'ab تعب
burden, hardship

ta'bān تعبان
exhausted, tired

mashrū' مشروع - مشارع
project, scheme, plan

Note the use of pronouns in the following sentences.

TRANSLATION	***MODEL SENTENCES***
1. He is a rich peasant.	١- هو فلاح غني.
2. This is a beautiful flower.	٢- هذه زهرة جميلة.
3. These are two beautiful roses.	٣- هاتان وردتان جميلتان.
4. These are expert engineers.	٤- هؤلاء مهندسون ماهرون.
5. These are female workers in the spinning factory.	٥- هؤلاء عاملات في مصنع النسيج.
6. That is the book without doubtful contents.	٦- ذلك الكتاب لاريب فيه.
7. That is a heavy tank.	٧- تلك دبابة ضخمة

8. Those are the accountants of the company. ٨- أولئك محاسبو الشركة.

9. She is a stewardess. ٩- هي مضيفى الطائرة.

10. He is a postman. ١٠- هو ساعي البـــريد.

11. They are two honest policemen. ١١- هما شرطيان أمينان.

12. They are nurses. ١٢- هن ممـــرضات.

13. The boy who succeeds in the examination is assiduous. ١٣- الولد الذي ينجح في الإمتحان مجتهد.

14. These are (the two) guests who visited us yesterday. ١٤- هذان الضيفان اللذان زارا بيتنا بالأمس.

LESSON TWELVE

Demonstrative and Relative Pronouns

الضمائر المتصلة وأسماء الإشارة والأسماء الموصولة

New York City

مَدِيْنَةُ نيوُيُورك

1. New York city is considered to be among the biggest and most famous cities of the world. It is one of the cities in the State of New York, and it is situated on the Eastern coast of the United States of America and on the shore of the Atlantic Ocean. The headquarters of the United Nations and the headquarters of the biggest international banks and the world's biggest stock exchange are found here.

١ –تُعتَبَرُ مَدِينَةُ نيوُيُورك مِن أكْبَر وأشْهَر المُدُن فِي العَالم. هِي إحْدَى مُدُن ولايةِ نيُويُورك وتَقَعُ عَلى السَّاحِلِ الشَّرقِي لِلولاياتِ الأمْرِيكِيّة المُتَّحدَة وتَقَعُ عَلى شَواطِئ المُحِيط الأطْلَنْطِي. وتُوجد فِيهَا مَقَرٌّ هَيئَة الأمَم المُتَّحدَة ومَراكِز أعظم البُنُوكِ الدولِيةِ وأشْهَر البُورصَات العَالمِيَة.

2. This city is considered to be one of the main centers in the world for cultural, economic and financial activities. It has a great number of libraries, famous theatres and many universities, colleges and institutes.

٢ – تُعْتَبَرُ هذِهِ المَدينَة مِن أهمِّ المَرَاكِز لِلنَّشَاطَاتِ الثَّقَافِيةِ والإقتِصَادِيَة والمَالِيةِ فِي العَالِم. وتحْتوِي عَلى مَكْتبَات عِدَّة ومَسَارح مَشهُورة والعَدِيد مِنَ الجَامِعَات والكُلِّيَّات والمَعَاهِد.

3. The residents of this city consist of ethnic groups who had emigrated to New York during the last centuries from all parts of the world. This concentration of numerous

٣ – يتَشَكَّلُ سُكَّان المَدِينَةِ مِن أقَلِّيَات قومِيَّةٍ هاجَرَتْ إليهَا خِلالَ القُرُون المَاضِيَّةِ مِن جَمِيع أنْحَاء العَالَم. أنَّ التَّجمُّع لِعَدِيدِ مِنَ الأقَلِّيَات فِي مَدِينَة

ethnic groups in New York has made it a center for various political, religious and social organizations.	نيُويُورك ضَمَنَ لـهَا أنْ تَكونَ مَركزا للمُنَظَمَات السِّيَاسِية والدِّينِيَّة والإِجْتِمَاعِيَّة المُتَنَوِّعَة.
4. Freedom in general and religious freedom in particular facilitate the co-existence of Churches, Synagogues and Mosques in all parts of the city.	٤- أنَّ الْحُرِّيّات الْعامَّة والدِّينِيَّة بِصِفة خَاصَّة قد أباح تَواجُد الْكَنَائِس والْمَعَابد وَالمَسَاجِدِ فِي جَمِيع أنْحَاء المَدِيْنَةِ.
5. More than the large buildings or its economic role in the world, what makes New York city so special is the unique ethnic diversity of its inhabitants.	٥- إنَّ عَظْمَة مَدِينَة نيُويُورك لَيستَ بِأبْنِيَتِها الشَّامِخَةِ أو دَورِهَا الإقْتِصَادي فِي العَالَم بَلْ هِيَ فِي التَّنَوُّع البَشَري مِن بَينِ سُكَّانِهَا

Those who study Arabic as a foreign language, are puzzled by combinations of inseparable pronouns, inseparable prepositions and conjunctions. They are called inseparable, because they are part of the word and are either prefixed or suffixed to it. When these pronouns, prepositions and conjunctions (indicated by a single letter or more) are joined to the word, they pose a problem for the beginner. But this problem ceases to exist as the student gets familiar with the language.

	Split	*Expression*
in the name of God	ب + اسم الله	بسم الله
his pen	قلم + ه	قلمه
your book	كتاب + ك	كتابك
in it	في + ه	فيه
and he wrote it	ف + كتب + ه	فكتبه

The pronouns that are attached الضَّمائِر المتَّصِلَة

Suffixed to Prepositions	Suffixed to nouns	Meaning	Mere suffixes	
				3rd per. m
لــهُ**	كِتَــابُهُ*	him : his	١. هُ	غائب مذكر
لهُمَــا	كتابهمــا	them : their	٢. هُما	
لهــم	كتابهــم	them : their	٣. هُم	
				3rd per. f
لهَــا	كتابهــا	her	٤. هَــا	غائب مؤنث
لهُمَــا	كتابهمــا	them : their	٥. هُما	
لهُــنَّ	كتابهــن	them : their	٦. هُن	
				2nd per. m
لــكَ	كتابــكَ	you : your	٧. كَ	مخاطب مذكر
لكمَــا	كتابكمــا	you : your	٨. كُما	
لكــم	كتابكــم	you : your	٩. كُم	
				2nd per. f
لــكِ	كتابــكِ	you : your	١٠. كِ	مخاطب مؤنث
لكمَــا	كتابكمــا	you : your	١١. كُما	
لكُــن	كتابُكُــنَّ	you : your	١٢. كُنَّ	
				1st per. m / f
لي	كتابــي	me : my	١٣. كَ	متكلم مذكر
لنَــا	كتابنــا	us : our	١٤. كُما	ومؤنث

---

* كتابه (كتاب + ه) his book

** لــه (ل + ه) for him

When a personal pronoun is the direct object of a verb it is attached to it. e.g.

I saw her. رأيتها *I struck him.* ضربته

Demonstrative Pronouns أسماء الإشارة

أسماء الإشارة *Demonstrative pronouns,* as in English, have separate words for near objects and distant objects. But in Arabic the demonstrative pronouns should agree with the gender and number of the person or object. e.g.

This is a useful book.	هــذا كِتــابٌ نــافِــعٌ
This is a spacious room.	هــذه حجــرة واسعة
These are expert craftsmen.	هؤلاء صناع ماهرون

For distant objects		For near objects			
Plural	Singular[1]	Plural	Dual	Singular	
أولئــك	**ذلك	هؤلاء	هذان	*هذا	m
أولئــك	تلك	هؤلاء	هاتان	هذه	f

Relative Pronouns الأسماء الموصولــة

		Plural	Dual	Singular	
Who; whom; that; which:	الذي	الذِين	اللذان	الذي	m
Who:	مَنْ	اللاتي	اللتان	التي	f
What; what thing:	مَا				

that **ذلك this *هذا

1. The dual form exists but it is not commonly used for distant objects.

VOCABULARY

qalīl قليل
a small number

aqalliya أقليــة
minority

kaṯīr كثير
many, abundant

akṯariya اكثرية
majority

qaum قوم : شعب
nation, race, people

hajara هجر
to emigrate, keep away

sakana سكن ؛ يسكن
to reside, to be still

sākin ساكن – سكان
resident, inhabitant

ḥāja حاجة
need, want

zāda زاد ؛ يزيد
to increase

ziyāda زيادة : اضافة
increase, addition

i'tibār اعتبار
consideration, outlook

I'tibāran min اعتبارا من
effective from

mauqi' موقع
situation, location

mutawaqqa' متوقع
expected, anticipated

tashkīl تشكيل
formation, building up

tanawwu' تنــوع
diversity, multiplicity

ittiḥād اتحاد
union, harmony

'adad عدد
number, figure

dāḵil داخل
inside, interior

dāḵili داخلي
internal

ḵārij خارج
outside, abroad

zaid زائد
excessive

barid بريد
post, mail

sāi'al barid ساعي البريد
the postman

ṭāba' طابع – طوابع
stamp, print

barq برق
lightning, flash

barqiya برقية : تلغراف
telegram

hātif : lasilki هاتف : لا سلكي
telephone, wireless

jara جرى ؛ يجري
to run, to flow

fasih فسيح
wide, spacious

nasaja نسج ؛ ينسج
to weave

mansaj منسج
weaving factory

nasama نسم : نسم
person (in census)

k̲āriji خارجي
external

rabaṭa ربط ؛ يربط
to bind, connect

rābiṭa رابطة – روابط
connection, league

munaẓẓama منظمة
organization

minā ميناء – موان
harbor

maḥaṭṭa محطة
station

sikkat al ḥadīd سكة الحديد
railway

maṭār مطار : محطة الطيران
airport

ṭāira طائرة
airplane

dabbāba دبابة
tank

sayyāra سيارة
automobile, car

sayyāra ujra سيارة أجرة : تكسي
taxi

ʻaāṣima عاصمة – عواصم
capital city, metropolis

wilāya ولاية
state, district

taftīsh تفتيش : فحص
investigation

mufattish مفتش
supervisor, inspector

ḥamala حمل ؛ يحمل
to carry

ḥammāl حمـال
porter

nazala نزل ؛ ينزل
to step down

ams أمس : البارحة
yesterday

al-yauma اليوم – أيام
today

ḡad غدا
tomorrow

imtiḥān إمتحان
examination

maza : maiz ميز ؛ يميز
to separate, set aside

shāḥina شاحنة
lorry

ḍak̲m ضخم
huge, big

ḥisāb حساب
calculation, accounting

ʻilmul ḥisāb علم الحساب
arithmetic

muḥāsib محاسب
accountant

mariḍa مرض ؛ يمرض
to get sick

marīḍ مريض
sick person

mumarriḍa ممرضة
nurse

mausim موسم
season, festival

mausimmi موسمي
seasonal

ṭaqs طقس : جو
climate

bard برد : برودة
cold, coldness

suqūt	سقوط	ḥarr	حر : حرارة
fall, crash, slip		*hot, heat*	
saqata	سقط ؛ يسقط	fākiha	فاكهة – فواكه
to fall down, drop		*fruit*	
k̲aḍrawāt	خضروات	ḍaḥiya	ضاحية – ضواحي
vegetables, greens		*outskirts, vicinity*	
ḥadīqa	حديقة : بستان	shadīd	شديد : عنيف
garden		*severe, hard*	
nabt	نبت – نبات	mumtāz	ممتاز : متميز
plant		*distinguished, notable*	

Note the use of pronouns in the following sentences:

TRANSLATION	*MODEL SENTENCES*
1. This student is active.	١– هذا الطالب نشيط
2. This is a tent of the army.	٢– هذه خيمة المعسكر
3. These are two faithful friends.	٣– هذان صديقان وفيان.
4. These are the students of the Arab Republic of Egypt.	٤– هؤلاء تلاميذ جمهورية مصر العربيـــة
5. That (person) is a journalist.	٥– ذلك صحافي
6. These (two) are doctors.	٦– هذان طبيبان
7. These (persons) are the leaders of the nation.	٧– اولئك زعماء القوم
8. He is the Defense Minister.	٨– هو وزير الدفاع
9. She is a girl scout.	٩– هي كشافة
10. They (two) are authors.	١٠– هما مصنفان.

LESSON THIRTEEN

Interrogatives — أدوات الإستفهام

Conversation — مُحَـــادثــــة

Shaik: Peace be with you.	الشيخ: السلام عليكــم
Young man: Peace be with you, welcome.	الفتى: وعليكم السلام، أهلا وسهلا
1. Sh: What is your name?	١. ش: ما اسمك؟
Y : My name is Abu Bakr.	ف: اسمي أبوبكــر
2. Sh: How old are you?	٢. ش: من عمرك؟
Y : I am twenty years old.	ف: عمري عشرون سنة.
3. Sh: Are you studying in the university?	٣. ش: أ أنت فـــي الجامعـــة؟
Y : Yes. I am at the University of Cairo.	ف: نعم. أنا في جامعة القاهرة
4. Sh: Which faculty did you join?	٤. ش: في أي كلية دخلت؟
Y : I have joined the faculty of engineering.	ف: دخلت في كليـــة الـهندسة
5. Sh: How many faculties are there at the university?	٥. ش: كم كلية في الجامعـــة
Y : The university has many faculties. Faculty of Medicine, Pharmacology, Science, Arts, Economics, Commerce and Law. And each faculty has different departments.	ف: في الجامِعَة كُليَات كَثِيرَة فيها كُلّيَة الطّبّ وكُلّيَة الصَّيدَلِية وكُلّيَة العُلُوم وكُلّيَة الآدَاب وكُلّية الإقتِصَاد وكُلّيَة التِّجَارة وكُلّيَة الحُقُوق وفِي كُل كُلّيَة أقسامٌ مُخْتَلِفة

6.	Sh: Are there students from other countries?	ش: هل في الجَامِعةِ طَلَبَة مِنْ بِلادٍ أُخْرَى؟	.٦
	Y: Yes, there are students from many countries at the university.	ف: نعم. بِالجَامِعَةِ طَلَبَــةَ مِنْ بِلادٍ كَثِيْرَةٍ	
7.	Sh: When do you (usually) go to the faculty?	ش: متَى تَذْهَبُ إِلى الْكُلِّيَّــةِ؟	.٧
	Y : I go at 8 a.m.	ف: أَذْهَبُ غِلَى الْكُلِّيَّةِ فِي السَّاعَــةِ الثَّامِنَةِ صَبَاحــاً	
8.	Sh:What are your hobbies?	ش: ما هُو هوايتكَ؟	.٨
	Y : I correspond and exchange stamps with friends here and abroad.	ف: أتَبَادَلُ الرَّسَائِل والطَّوَابع مَعَ اَصْدِقَائي فِي دَاخِلَ البِلَد وَخَارِجِها	
9.	Sh: How many lectures you attend every day?	ش: كَمْ مُحَاضَرَة تَأخُذُ فــِي اليَومِ؟	.٩
	Y : I attend six lectures.	ف: آخُذُ ستَّ مَحَاضَرَات	
10.	Sh: Where do you go in the evening after you return home?	ش: أينَ تَذْهَبُ فِي الْمَسَاءِ بَعْدَ رُجُوعِك إِلى الْبَيْتِ؟	.١٠
	Y : I go to the central library or visit friends.	ف: اَذْهَبُ إِلى المكتبة المركزيةِ أو أزور أصدقائي	
11.	Sh: Do you go by car or do you walk?	أ تَذْهَبُ رَاكِباً فِي السَّيَّارةِ امْ مَاشِيــاً؟	.١١
	Y : Sometimes I go by car, sometimes I walk.	ف: أذْهَبُ رَاكِباً فِي السَّيَّارةِ أحْياناً وَمَاشِياً أحْياناً أخْرَى.	

12. Sh: I wish you success. ١٢. ش: أتَمَنّى لكَ النَّجَاح والتَّوفِيق.

Y : Thanks. Good-bye. ف: شكرا – إلي اللّقــاء

Interrogative sentences are introduced by the Particles هَلْ or أ ; أ precedes the first word of the interrogative sentence. In sentences Nos. 3 and 11, أ precedes a pronoun and a verb respectively. In certain cases interrogative pronouns and adverbs are also used for making interrogative sentences.

Interrogative Pronouns		Adverbs which are widely used as interrogatives		Interrogative Particles	
Who?	مَنْ	How?	كَيْفَ	Is?	هَـلْ
What?	مَـا	When?	مَتَى	Are?	
What?	مَاذَا	Where?	أيْـنَ	Do?	أ
What? Which?	أيٌّ	Why?	لِمَاذَا	Have?	
What? Which? (f)	أيَّـةُ	How many/ How much?	كَـمْ		

VOCABULARY

raja'a	رجَع ؛ يرجع	baḍ al aḥyān	بعض الأحيان
to return		*sometimes*	
murāja'a	مُراجَعَة	ṣaḥiba	صحب ؛ يصحب
revision, verification		*to accompany*	
rujū'	رجــوع : عودة	qabl	قبــل
return		*before*	

mādda مادة – مواد
material, component

adat أداة – أدوات
tool, instrument

baḥr بحـــر : محيط
sea, ocean

shaṭṭ شط
shore, coast

shaṭi al baḥr شاطئ البحر
sea coast

masha مشى ؛ يمشي
to walk

māshi ماش : ماشية
pedestrian, cattle

sibāha سباحة : عوم
swimming

fahima فهم : أدرك
to understand

istifhām إستفهام
inquiry, act of inquiring

ḥādit حادث – حوادث
accident, event, mishap

ḥaddata حدّث : روى
to narrate

b'adu بعــد
after

al-ān الآن
now

shahida شهد ؛ يشهد
to be present, to give testimony

raa رأي : أبصر
to see, observe

marra مرة – مرارا
once

aḥyānan أحيانا
occasionally

ʒ āda جاد : جود : حَسُن
to improve

qasama قسم : تقسيم
to divide, partition

qisma قسمة
fate, division

qism قسم – أقسام
department, section

ḥaraka حركة – حركات
movement

ta'allama تعلــم
to learn

hadit حديث

new, news

bain بيــن

between

shaik شيخ - شيوخ

elderly person

fata فتى : شاب

youth

ahlan wa sahlan أهلا وسهلا: مرحبا

welcome

in sha' Allah إن شاء الله

God willing

Ma saha' Allah ما شاء الله

God intended, amazing

fi aman Allah في أمان الله

in the protection of God

ba'ata بعث ؛ يبعث

to send

bait باعث

motive, cause

mab'ut مبعوث

delegate, envoy

wafd وفد : بعثة

delegation, deputation

hal حال : حالــة

state, condition

hamida حمد ؛ يحمد

to praise

alhamdu li Allah الحمد لله

praise be to God

akar آخر

another, one more

akir أخير

last, latest

akkara أخّر : تأخّر

to delay

muta'akkir متــأخّر

late, delayed

mubakkir مبكر

early

qada قضى

to spend time, to finish

shai, amr شيء : أمر

thing, matter

jaa, ata جاء : اتى

to come, arrive

tarik تاريخ

date, history

yamīn يمين : اليد اليمنى
the right hand

yasār يسار : اليد اليسرى
the left hand

qabīla قبيلة : عشيرة
tribe

ḥaql حقل – حقول
field

natīja نتيجة : حاصل
result, product

intāj إنتاج
production, output

naḥwa نحو : اتجاه
side, direction

qāla قال ؛ يقول
to say

qawl قول
statement

rabb رب
Lord

fa'ala فعل ؛ يفعل
to do, perform

mīlad ميلاد – مواليد
birth, birthday

bidāya بداية
beginning, start

nihāya نهاية
termination, end

'uṭla عطلة
leisure, vacation

mu'aṭṭal معطل
out of order, inoperative

ujra أجرة
hire, rent, fee

jug̲rāfiya جغرافية
geography

ṣādiq صادق
truthful, true

t̲aman ثمن : قيمة
price, cost

g̲ālin غال
costly, dear

rak̲īs رخيص
cheap, low

Make a note of the interrogatives in the following sentences:

	TRANSLATION	*MODEL SENTENCES*
1.	What is that in your right hand O Moses?	١- وما تلك بيمينك يا موسى؟
2.	From which tribe are you?	٢- مِن أيِّ قبيلَة أنتَ؟
3.	Are you hungry?	٣- أ أنتَ جَائِــع؟
4.	Do you have a watch?	٤- هلْ عِندَك ساعَة؟
5.	Where is the zoological garden?	٥- أينَ حَدِيقَة الْحَيوَانات؟
6.	How many cows are there in the field?	٦- كمْ بقَرَة فِي الحَقْل؟
7.	How many students are there in your school?	٧- كَم تِلمِيذا فِي مَدرَستِك
8.	What is the result of your examination?	٨- ما نَتِيجَة اِمتِحَانِك؟
9.	What are our duties towards our nation?	٩- ما وَاجِبُنا نَحوَ وطَنِك؟
10.	What did your teacher say?	١٠-مـاذَا قال استَاذُك؟
11.	Is your brother in the school?	١١-هلْ اخُوك فِي المَدرَسة؟
12.	Which book is with you?	١٢-أي كِتاب معَك؟
13.	Why did you go to Rabat?	١٣-لِماذَا ذهَبتَ الى الرَّباط؟
14.	When do you return from the college?	١٤-متى ترجعُ من الكُلّيَة؟
15.	How is your health?	١٥-كَيف صِحَّتك؟
16.	Which of the favors of your Lord would you deny then?	١٦-فَبِأيِّ آلآءِ رَبكُمَا تُكَذِّبَان؟
17.	Why are you traveling?	١٧-لماذَا تُسَافِر؟
18.	What is the price of this book?	١٨-كَم ثَمَن هذَا الكِتَاب؟
19.	Has the news of the army come to you?	١٩-هل آتاك حَدِيث الجُنُود؟

19. Has the news of the army come to you?	١٩-هل أتاك حَدِيث الجُنُود؟
20. What is the benefit of iron?	٢٠-ما فَائِدَة الحَدِيد؟
21. What is the capital of Lebanon?	٢١-ما عاصِمَة لبنَان؟
22. Who are those men?	٢٢-من هؤلاءِ الرِّجال؟
23. How many days are there in a year?	٢٣-كم يوما فِي السَّنَة؟
24. Is the watchman honest?	٢٤-هل الحَارس أمِين؟
25. When do you play?	٢٥-متى تَلْعب؟
26. Why are you late?	٢٦-لِمَاذا أنْت مُتَأخِّر؟
27. How did you spend yesterday?	٢٧-كيف قضَيتَ أمْس؟
28. What is that you are having?	٢٨-أي شيءٍ عِندَك؟
29. Where is your bicycle?	٢٩-أينَ درَّاجَتُك؟
30. When is your examination?	٢٠-مَتى إمْتِحَانُك؟
31. What has taken place yesterday?	٣١-مَاذا حَدَثَ أمس؟

LESSON FOURTEEN

Prepositions — حروف الجر

The Village — القرية

1. The entire village is full of activity and liveliness and its people are happy.	١- القريةُ كُلُّها عمل ونَشاطٌ وأهلُهَا فِي فرح.
2. The peasant is happy with the cultivation of rice.	٢- الفَلاحُ سعيدٌ بزَرْعِ الأرُزْ.
3. It is an important (source of) income for him and he depends on it.	٣- لأنَّه مَحصُولٌ هَامٌ له ويُعْتَمَد عليهِ.
4. He sells it and buys from the profit things he heeds for a living.	٤- يَبِيعُه ويَشْتَري حَاجَتَه مِن ثَمَنِه.
5. The peasant works in the field.	٥- يعمَلُ الفَلاّحُ فِي الْحَقِل
6. His sons are at his right and his brother is to his left. His wife is sitting on a rock and with her is the food (packet). And around her are the cattle.	٦- وأبْنَاؤهُ عَن يَمِينِهِ وأخُوهُ عَن يَسَارهِ وزَوجَتُهُ جَالِسَة عَلى صَخْرَةٍ وَفِي يَدِهَا الطَّعَامُ ومَن حَولِهَا البَهائِمُ (المَواشِي).
7. This family is busy from morning till sunset.	٧- هذِه الأسْرَة تَشْتَغِلُ مِنَ الصَّبَاح غلِي غُرُوبِ الشَّمْس.

The prepositions are called حروف الجر. The word followed by the preposition is called مجرُور, and the preposition with its noun is known as الجَار والمَجْرُور.

Prepositions are:

(a) Separable prepositions e.g. فِي *in* (see sentence No.1)

(b) Inseparable prepositions e.g. ب *by, with* بــزرع (see sentence No.2)

Nouns followed by prepositions are in the "genitive case" i.e. مجرور, they end with ـــ which is the sign of the genitive case.

VOCABULARY

'aliy	علي : عال	aktubu	أكتب
high, exalted		*I write*	
sufl	سفل : أسفل	'amdan	عمدا
low, lowest		*intentionally*	
t̲arwa	ثروة : غنى	ijbar	إجبار
riches, wealth		*compulsion*	
'usfur	عصفور : طير	qarya	قرية
a small bird, sparrow		*village*	
tawula	طاولة	fariha	فرح ؛ يفرح
table		*to be glad*	
ibta'ada	إبتعد ؛ يبتعد	farhan	فرحــان
to avoid		*delightful, gay*	
k̲atar	خطر	sa'yeed	سعيــد
danger, risk		*lucky, happy*	
'ada	عاد : رجع	mahzun	محزون
to return		*sad*	
'itamada	اعتمد ؛ يعتمد	urzz	أرز : رز
to rely		*rice*	

'imād عماد : عمد
pillar, support

'itimād اعتماد
reliance, credit

jarama جرم
to commit a crime

mujrim مجرم
criminal

nār نار : حريقة
fire

sūq سوق - أسواق
market

'afw عفو : عفاء
pardon

'afwan عفوا
I beg your pardon

miṣ'ad مصعد
lift, elevator

darj درج
staircase

jāiza جائزة - جوائز
reward, prize

ishtağala اشتغل
to keep busy

ḥaṣala حصل
to collect

maḥṣūl محصول
product, yield

mula' مولع
fond of, in love with

shafa شفى
to cure

mustashfa, 'iyāda مستشفى:عيادة
hospital, clinic

is'āf إسعاف
medical service, ambulance

ibn ابن - أبناء
son

bint بنت - بنات
daughter

zawj زوج - أزواج
husband

zawja زوجة
wife

tazawwaja تزوج
to marry

kull wāhid كل واحد
each one

mashḡūl مشغول
busy

ṣabāḥ صباح
morning

ṣabāḥ al ḵair صباح الخير
good morning

masā مساء
evening

masā al ḵair مساء الخير
good evening

sijn سجن
prison

ṣayd صيد
hunting

ṣayyād صياد : صائد
hunter

siyāḥa, safar سياحة : سفر
tour, journey

sayyāḥ سياح
tourist

aḏina أذن : سمح
to permit

iḏn, ruḵṣa إذن : رخصة
permission, license

bahīma بهيمة – بهائم
beasts, animals

usra أسرة
family

jasad : jism جسد : جسم
body

rūḥ : nafs روح : نفس
soul, spirit

mu'āraḍa معارضة
opposition

'itirāḍ اعتراض
objection

ẓahr ظهر
back, rear side

ḡadiba غضب ؛ يغضب
to be angry

ḡaḍbān غضبان : زعلان
angry

darj درج
cupboard, locker

safīh سفيه : أحمق
foolish

maḥkama محكمة
court, tribunal

	TRANSLATION	*MODEL SENTENCES*
1.	The teacher is in the class.	١- الأستاذ في الفصلْ
2.	The upper hand is better than the lower (receiving) hand.	٢- اليَد العُليا خير من اليد السُفْلى
3.	Knowledge is better than wealth.	٣- العلم خير من الثروة
4.	The sparrow is on the tree.	٤- العصفور علي الشجر
5.	The book is on the table.	٥- الكتاب علي الطاولة
6.	The wise (person) keeps himself at a distance from danger.	٦- العاقل يبتعد عن الخطر
7.	The minister returned to the capital.	٧- عاد الوزير الي العاصمة
8.	I write with my pen.	٨- أكتب بقلمي
9.	Do not play with fire.	٩- لا تلعب بالنار
10.	There are two gates for the college and there is a watchman at each.	١٠-للكلية بابان وعلي كل باب حارس
11.	I saw a parrot in the cage.	١١-رأيت ببغاء في القفص
12.	The policeman is getting down from the horse.	١٢-ينزل الشرطي عن الحصان
13.	The generous (person) forgives the wicked.	١٣-الكريم يعفو عن المسيئ
14.	This key is for my room.	١٤-هذا المفتاح لغرفتي.
15.	The reward is for the winner.	١٥-الجائزة للفائز
16.	The patient is in the hospital.	١٦-المريض في المستشفى
17.	The criminal is in the prison.	١٧-المجرم في السجن

18. The saddle is on the horse's back. ١٨-السرج علي ظهر الفرس

19. The teacher was angry with the student. ١٩-غضب الأستاذ علي التلميذ

20. Heat comes from the sun. ٢٠-تـــأتي الحرارة من الشمس

21. I travelled from Basra to Baghdad. ٢١-سافرت من البصرة الى بغداد

22. He is fond of hunting. ٢٢-هو مولع بالصيــد

23. The tourist returned to his country. ٢٣-عاد السائح الى بلده

24. I hear with my ear. ٢٤-أسمع بأذني

LESSON FIFTEEN

Verbal Sentence – The Past Tense
الجملة الفعلية - الفعل الماضـــي

Sayeed and his Friend / سعيد وصديـــقـــه

1. Sayeed returned from school and placed his bag on the table.

١- رجع سعيد مِن المَدرَسَةِ وَوَضَـــعَ حَقِيْبَتَه عَلى الطَّاوِلَةِ.

2. Then he washed his face, ate lunch and drank tea.

٢- ثُمَّ غَسَلَ وَجْهَـــه وتَنَــاوَلَ وَجْبَـــةَ الغَداء وشَرِبَ الشَّاي.

3. He went out of the house for recreation and arrived at the house of his friend, William.

٣- وخَرَجَ مِن البَيْتِ لِلنُّزْهَةِ وَوَصَـــلَ الى مَنْزِلَ صَدِيقِه وليم.

4. Then the two friends went to the industrial exhibition and saw a variety of industrial products. They (two) returned after purchasing a television set.

٤- ثُمَّ ذَهبَ الصَّدِيقَـــانِ الى المَعْـــرِض الصِّنَاعِي وَشَـــاهَدَا أنْواعـــاً مِـــن المُنْتَجَاتِ الصِّنَاعِيَّةِ وَعادَا بَعْـــدَ أنْ إشْتَرَيَا جِهَازًا تِلْفِزْيُونِيـــاً.

5. But Sayeed's sister went to the kitchen and helped her mother with cooking.

٥- لَكِنْ أخْتُ سَعِيد ذَهَبَتْ الى المَطْبَـــخ وسَاعَدَتْ أمَّهَا في الطَّبْخ.

6. Her father returned from the market, in his hand was a basket, full of vegetables and fruits.

٦- ورجَعَ أَبُوها مِن السُّوق وفِي يَـــدِهِ سَلَّة مَمْلُوءةً بِالخَضْرِ و الفاكِهَةِ.

7. Zainab saw her father and she hurried towards him and took the basket from him.

٧-رأتْ زَينَب أباها فأسْـــرَعت إليـــهِ وأخَذَتِ السَّلَّة مِنْـــهُ.

8. The father was happy with Zainab for her love for him.

٨-فرِحَ الأبُ بِزَيْنَبَ لِحُبِّها لهُ.

9. The mother brought supper and all of them sat around the dining table. The family ate supper and thanked God for His bounty.	٩-وأحْضَرَتِ الأمُّ الْعَشَاء فجَلَسُوا جَمِيْعاً حَوْلَ الْمَائِدَة وَتَنَاوَلَت الأسْرَةُ الْعَشَاء وَشَكَرُوا اللهَ عَلَى نِعَمِهِ.

Verb : An Introduction

A sentence which begins with a verb is called الجملة الفعلية *"the verbal sentence".* The verb consists of three root or radical letters, e.g. فعل *to do* كتب *to write.* These are called triliteral verbs. But there are some quadriliteral verbs too, like دحرج *to push,* which consist of four radical letters.

To know the radical letters of any given verb is essential in order to find it in the Arabic dictionaries. Take for instance the word فعل which consists of (1) ف (2) ع (3) ل.

(1)	ف	is called	فاء الكلمة	*the first radical*
(2)	ع	is called	عين الكلمة	*the second radical*
(3)	ل	is called	لام الكلمة	*the third radical*

(The three radicals are derived from المصدر *verbal root*)

Remember that in all books of Arabic grammar, the verb فعل and its derivatives are used as patterns for all verbs whether triliteral or quadriliteral and their derivatives.

Arabic dictionaries list the verb in the third person singular masculine, simple perfect, active, its derivatives follow. Further the meaning given would be in the infinitive. e.g.

فعـــل *to do,* نظر *to see* whereas the actual meaning of فعل is *he did* and that of نظر *he saw.*

The Arab grammarians have divided the verbs into three categories:

(1) the Perfect, denoting a completed action الفعل الماضي

(2) the Imperfect denoting an incomplete action الفعل المضارع

(3) the Imperative (which includes the Negative) الفعل الأمر

Agreement between the Verb and Subject:

The principal rules relating to the agreement between فعل *verb* and its فاعل *subject* are as follows:

(a) When the فعل *verb* precedes the subject:

(1) If the فاعل *subject* is masculine, or dual or plural, the verb will be in the 3rd person singular masculine. e.g.

Sayeed returned رجــع سعيــد

The two (male) friends went ذهَبَ الصَّدِيقــان

Many men went ذهَبَ الرِّجَــال

(2) If the فاعل *subject* is feminine singular or dual or plural, the verb will be in the 3rd person singular feminine. E.g.

Sayeed's sister went. ذهبت أخت سعيــد

The two girls went. ذهَبَت البنتــان

Many girls went. ذهَبَت البنــات

(3) If الفاعل *the subject* is a collective noun, the verb may be in the 3rd person singular, masculine or feminine. e.g.

The family ate supper. تنَاولَت الأسرةُ طعام العشَــاء

(b) If the الفاعل *the subject* comes before الفعل *the verb*, the verb must agree with it in gender and number. e.g.

The two (male) friends witnessed.	الصدِيقان شاهدَا
Many boys witnessed.	الأولاد شــاهدوا
Many girls witnessed.	البنات شاهدن

Vowels of the second radical:

In the active voice, the first and the third radicals of verbs in the past tense, will have ـَـ, while the second radical may have either of the three vowel signs ـَـ ـُـ ـِـ. These three types of verbs are illustrated below:

نَصَرَ	ضَرَبَ	جَلَسَ	دَخَلَ	فَتَحَ	*فَعَلَ	١.
to help	*to strike*	*to sit*	*to enter*	*to open*		
لَبِسَ	شَهِدَ	حَسِبَ	سَمِعَ	شَرِبَ	*فَعِلَ	٢.
to wear	*to see*	*to suppose*	*to hear*	*to drink*		
ضَعُفَ	كَبُرَ	قَرُبَ	بَعُدَ	كَرُمَ	*فَعُلَ	٣.
to grow weak	*to grow*	*to be near*	*to be distant*	*to be generous*		

Note: When a verb in the past tense is converted into the future tense, the vowel of the second radical remains the same in some verbs, and changes in others.

---

* *verbal pattern*

Conjugation of the Past Tense:

			Suffixes	غائب مذكر			**3rd Per. Mas.**
كَرُمَ	سَمِعَ	نَصَرَ		He did	فَعَلَ	١	Sing.
كَرُمَا	سَمِعَا	نَصَرَا	ا	They both did	فَعَلاَ	٢	Dual
كَرُمُوا	سَمِعُوا	نَصَرُوا	وا	They (all) did	فَعَلُوا	٣	Plural
				غائب مؤنث			**3rd Per. Fem.**
كَرُمَتْ	سَمِعَتْ	نَصَرَتْ	تْ	She did	فَعَلَتْ	٤	Sing.
كَرُمَتَا	سَمِعَتَا	نَصَرَتَا	تَا	They both did	فَعَلَتَا	٥	Dual
كَرُمْنَ	سَمِعْنَ	نَصَرْنَ	نَ	They (all) did	فَعَلْنَ	٦	plural
				مخاطب مذكر			**2nd Per. Mas.**
كَرُمْتَ	سَمِعْتَ	نَصَرْتَ	تَ	You did	فَعَلْتَ	٧	Sing.
كَرُمْتُمَا	سَمِعْتُمَا	نَصَرْتُمَا	تُمَا	You both did	فَعَلْتُمَا	٨	Dual
كَرُمْتُمْ	سَمِعْتُمْ	نَصَرْتُمْ	تُمْ	You (all) did	فَعَلْتُمْ	٩	Plural
				مخاطب مؤنث			**2nd Per. Fem.**
كَرُمْتِ	سَمِعْتِ	نَصَرْتِ	تِ	You did	فَعَلْتِ	١٠	Sing.
كَرُمْتُمَا	سَمِعْتُمَا	نَصَرْتُمَا	تُمَا	You both did	فَعَلْتُمَا	١١	Dual
كَرُمْتُنَّ	سَمِعْتُنَّ	نَصَرْتُنَّ	تُنَّ	You (all) did	فَعَلْتُنَّ	١٢	Plural
				متكلم مذكر و مؤنث			**1st Per. Mas./Fem.**
كَرُمْتُ	سَمِعْتُ	نَصَرْتُ	تُ	I did	فَعَلْتُ	١٣	Sing.
كَرُمْنَا	سَمِعْنَا	نَصَرْنَا	نَا	We did	فَعَلْنَا	١٤	Plural

الْمَـــاضِي الْقرِيْـــب " The near past" is formed by the addition of قدْ to الفِعْل الْمَاضِي. e.g.

He has gone. قَـــدْ ذَهَبَ

He has heard. قَـــدْ سَمِعَ

The past negative is formed by adding مَـــا to the tense. e.g.

He did not go. مَا ذَهِبَ

He did not hear. مَا سَمِعَ

1. The Verb, like the personal pronouns, has three persons:

   1. First person *the speaker* المُتَكَلّم
   2. Second person *the individual spoken to* المُخَاطَب
   3. Third person *the individual spoken of* الغَائِب

2. The endings in the conjugation are simply shortened forms of personal pronouns used as nominative.

3. When a personal pronoun is the direct object of a verb it is attached to it as a suffix. e.g.

   I love you أحِبُّك

   I sent them out أخْرَجتُهمْ

4. A peculiar feature of the Arabic language is its comprehensiveness. What is conveyed in a sentence in other languages is sometimes expressed in one single word in Arabic. (see the above examples)

VOCABULARY

ak̲ada أخذ ؛ يأخذ

to take, to receive

aḥḍara أحضر : جاء به

to bring, to fetch

waḍa'a وضع ؛ يضع

to put down, to give birth to

jamī'an جميعا : الجميع

all, entirety

jamā'a جماعة

group of people

jam'iya جمعية : إتحاد

association

tanāwala تناول الطعام

to take food

nāla نال ؛ ينال

to obtain

bāi' بائع

seller, salesman

ma'bad معبد

place of worship

d̲akara ذكر

to remember, to mention

ḥaqība حقيبة : شمطة

bag, suitcase

fuṭūr فطور : أكل الصباح

breakfast

'ashā عشاء

dinner, supper

ḡada غذاء : طعام الظهر

lunch

iḡtasala إغتسل ؛ يغتسل

to bathe

ḥalīb حليب : لبن

milk

qahwa قهوة

coffee

shāy شاي

tea

k̲araja خرج ؛ يخرج

to go out

nuzha نزهة

excursion, recreation

ḡādara غادر ؛ يغادر

to depart

da'ā دعا
to call

da'wa دعوة
invitation, propoganda

ḥafla حفلة
social gathering, reception

ḥaflat al-shāy حفلة الشاي
tea party

salla سلة
basket

sallat almuhmālat سلة المهملات
waste-paper basket

ḥarasa حرس ؛ يحرس
to watch, to guard

ḥāris حارس
watchman

dajjāja دجاجة
hen

bāḍat باضت الدجاجة
the hen laid eggs

baiḍa بيضة - بيض
egg

nabaḥa al kalb نبح الكلب
the dog barked

waṣala وصل ؛ يصل
to reach

wuṣūl وصول
arrival, receipt

manzil : bait منزل : بيت
residence, house

'araḍa عرض ؛ يعرض
to display, to offer

ma'raḍ معرض
exhibition, showroom

nau' نوع - أنواع
variety, sort

ṭabaḵa طبخ الطعام
to cook food

ṭabbāḵ طباخ
cook

maṭbaḵ مطبخ
kitchen

sā'ada ساعد
to help, to assist

sā'iq سائق
driver, pilot

zamīl زميل - زملاء
companion, colleague

zā'ra al asad زأر الأسد

The lion roared.

ṣāḥa ad-dīk صاح الديك

cock's crow

'amīd عميد – عمداء

principal, dean, chief

liṣṣ لص : سارق

thief

tallaq طلاق

divorce

aduw عدو – أعداء

enemy

riḥla رحلة : سفر

excursion, journey

ḥarīm حريم

sanctuary, harem, wife

ḥalāl حلال

permitted, legal

ḥarām حرام

prohibited, sin

mamnū' ممنوع

banned, forbidden

hilāl هلال

crescent

dawā دواء – أدوية

medicine

mamlū' مملوء

filled up, loaded

saṭr سطر : خط

line, row

arsala أرسل ؛ يرسل

to send, to forward

rasūl رسول – رسل

messenger, envoy

risāla رسالة : خطاب

message, letter

iltaqaṭa إلتقط ؛ يلتقط

to pick up

finā ad-dār فناء الدار

courtyard

nāfida نافذة : شباك

window

kura كرة

ball

kuratul qadam كرة القدم

soccer, football

mubārāt مبارات

match, contest

shammāʼa	شماعة	mashʼūm	مشئوم
hat and clothes rack		*unlucky, unfortunate*	
miḥrāṯ	محراث	mubārak	مبارك
plough		*lucky, fortunate*	
ʻallaqa	علــق	jarra	جر ؛ يجر
to attach, to hang		*to pull*	

TRANSLATION	***MODEL SENTENCES***
1. I saw eleven stars.	١- رأيت أحد عشر كوكبــا.
2. Marwan has written his lesson.	٢- قد كتب مروان درسه.
3. The peasant went to the field.	٣- ذهب الفلاح إلى الحقل.
4. The minister has left Beirut.	٤- قد غادر الوزير بيروت.
5. The teacher (f) reached Philadelphia.	٥- وصلت المعلمة فيلادلفيا.
6. The seller (f) of the flowers sat at the door of the temple.	٦- جلست بائعة الأزهار علــى باب المعبد.
7. I remembered my friend who traveled to Egypt.	٧- ذكرت صديقي الذي سافــر إلـــي مصر.
8. I invited my friends to a tea party.	٨- دعوت أصدقائي لحفلة الشاي.
9. The watchman placed the key in its place.	٩- وضع الحارس المفتاح فــي مكانــه
10. Rain fell from the sky.	١٠-نزل المطر من السماء.
11. The gardener picked the rose.	١١-قطف البستاني الوردة.
12. Khalid sent a letter to his people.	١٢-أرسل خالد رسالة إلي أهله

13. The student took the paper from country yard of the school and put it in the waste-paper basket. ١٣-إلتقط التلميذ ورقة من فناء المدرسة ووضعها في سلة المهملات.

14. The girls have passed the examination.. ١٤-البنات نجحن في الإمتحان.

15. The girl ate the apple. ١٥-أكلت البنت التفاحة.

16. The peasant cultivated sugarcane. ١٦-ورع الفلاح قصب السكر.

17. Tagore visited the United States. ١٧-زار تاغور الولايات المتحدة.

18. I listened to the advice of my teacher. ١٨-سمعت نصيحة أستاذي.

19. The dog barked at the thief. ١٩-نبح الكلب علي اللص.

20. The student opened his book. ٢٠-فتح التلميذ كتابه.

21. The Principal has returned from abroad ٢١-قد عاد العميد من الخارج

22. The soldier opened fire on the enemy. ٢٢-أطلق الجندي النار على العدو

23. Towfeek went for an excursion with his classmates. ٢٣-خرج توفيق في رحلة مع زملائه.

24. The sick man asked the nurse for medicine. ٢٤-طلب المريض الدواء من الممرضة.

25. The crescent appeared on the sky. ٢٦-ظهر الهلال في السماء.

26. The cock crew at dawn. ٢٦-صاح الديك في الفجر

27. Jowhar hung his clothes on the hanger. ٢٧-علق جوهر ملابسه علي الشماعة.

28. The two bulls pulled the plough. ٢٨-جر الثوران المحراث

29. My brother watched the football match. ٢٩-شاهد أخي مباراة كرة القدم.

LESSON SIXTEEN

Present and Future Tense

The Imperfect Tense الفعل المضارع

The River Nile نهر النيل

1. The Nile is one of the longest rivers in the world. Its valley is known for its fertility and abundance.

١-النيل من أطول أنهار الدنيا وواديه يمتاز بالخصب والرخاء.

2. People in ancient times did not know the sources of the Nile and they thought that it sprang from heaven.

٢-كان الناس قديما يجهلون منابع النيل ويظنون أنه ينبع من السماء.

3. In the last century its unknown sources were discovered. These are the three great lakes in the center of Africa.

٣-وفي القرن الماضي كشفت منابعه المجهولة وهي بحيرات ثلاث عظيمة في أواسط إفريقية.

4. Two large tributaries flow into the Nile: the Subaat and the Blue Nile. A small tributary also joins it, called the Atbara.

٤-يتصل بالنيل رافدان كبيران السوباط والنيل الأزرق ويتصل به أيضا رافد صغير هو عطبرة.

5. These three tributaries spring from the mountains of Ethiopia. Heavy rains fall on these mountains in summer, and these tributaries carry the water and (alluvial) soil to the Nile.

٥-وهذه الروافد الثلاث تنبع من جبال الحبشة - تسقط الأمطار الغزيرة صيفا علي هذه الجبال فتنقل الروافد المياه والغرين إلي النيل.

6. The Nile runs through the great desert and heads northwards until it flows into the Mediterranean Sea.	٦-ويخترق النيل الصحراء الكـــبرى ويتجه إلي الشمال حتى يصب فـــي البحر المتوسط.
7. An ancient civilization developed in the Nile Valley. And its remaining monuments bear witness of its majesty.	٧-وفي وادي النيل نشـــأت حضـــارة عريقة تشـــهد بعظمتـــها آثارهـــا الباقيـــة.

The Imperfect tense, **الفعل المضارع** expresses an action still incomplete and could mean either (1) Present and Present Continuous tenses or (2) Future Imperfect tense. The Imperfect tense is formed from the three radical letters of the past tense **الفعل المــاضي** and with the addition of one or more of these letters: ي , ن , ت , ا . These are known as "the signs of the Imperfect tense". From **كتب** *he wrote* (past tense) the following Imperfect tenses are formed.

نَكْتُبُ	أَكْتُبُ	يَكْتُبُ	تكتبُ
We are writing or will write	*I am writing or will write*	*He writes or will write*	*You are writing or will write*

Note that the first radical letter of the imperfect verb has no vowel mark, but is governed by the vowel of the sign of **مضارع** .

The number and gender of the person is expressed in the conjugation with the addition of ي , ن , ت , ا .

الفعل المضـــارع "The Imperfect" in itself denotes only unfinished action, but it may be used to indicate the future by putting the independent word **ســوف** before it, or by prefixing its contraction س (ســـ): e.g.

Zaid is writing or will write يكتب زيـــد

Zaid would write (in future) سيكتب زيد - سوف يكتب زيد

س is used to indicate "near future" and ســـوف is used for "distant future".

The vowel of the second radical of the Imperfect in respect of some verbs, will be the same as that of the past perfect. e.g.

Imperfect		Past
يَفْتَحُ	*to open*	١- فَتَحَ
يَكْرُمُ	*to be generous*	٢- كَرُمَ
يَحْسِبُ	*to suppose*	٣- حَسِبَ

But in some verbs, the vowel of the 2nd radical of the Imperfect المضارع is different from that of the second radical of the past perfect, المَاضي . e.g.

يَسْمَعُ	*to hear*	٤- سَمِعَ
يَنْصُرُ	*to help*	٥- نَصَرَ
يَضْرِبُ	*to strike*	٦- ضَرَبَ

The vowel of the second radical of the Imperfect is always shown in the dictionaries along with the meaning of the past perfect verb. The conjugation of the model verbs, given above, is as follows:

غائب مذكر

3rd Per. mas.

Sing.	يَفْتَحُ	يَكْرُمُ	يَحْسِبُ	يَسْمَعُ	يَنْصُرُ	يَضْرِبُ
Dual	يَفْتَحَانِ	يَكْرُمَانِ	يَحْسِبَانِ	يَسْمَعَانِ	يَنْصُرَانِ	يَضْرِبَانِ
Plural	يَفْتَحُونَ	يَكْرُمُونَ	يَحْسِبُونَ	يَسْمَعُونَ	يَنْصُرُونَ	يَضْرِبُونَ

غائب مؤنث

3rd Per. fem.

Sing.	تَفْتَحُ	تَكْرُمُ	تَحْسِبُ	تَسْمَعُ	تَنْصُرُ	تَضْرِبُ
Dual	تَفْتَحَانِ	تَكْرُمَانِ	تَحْسِبَانِ	تَسْمَعَانِ	تَنْصُرَانِ	تَضْرِبَانِ
Plural	يَفْتَحْنَ	يَكْرُمْنَ	يَحْسِبْنَ	يَسْمَعْنَ	يَنْصُرْنَ	يَضْرِبْنَ

مخاطب مذكر

2nd Per. mas.

Sing.	تَفْتَحُ	تَكْرُمُ	تَحْسِبُ	تَسْمَعُ	تَنْصُرُ	تَضْرِبُ
Dual	تَفْتَحَانِ	تَكْرُمَانِ	تَحْسِبَانِ	تَسْمَعَانِ	تَنْصُرَانِ	تَضْرِبَانِ
Plural	تَفْتَحُونَ	تَكْرُمُونَ	تَحْسِبُونَ	تَسْمَعُونَ	تَنْصُرُونَ	تَضْرِبُونَ

مخاطب مؤنث

2nd Per. fem.

Sing.	تَفْتَحِيْنَ	تَكْرُمِيْنَ	تَحْسَبِيْنَ	تَسْمَعِيْنَ	تَنْصُرِيْنَ	تَضْرِبِيْنَ
Dual	تَفْتَحَانِ	تَكْرُمَانِ	تَحْسِبَانِ	تَسْمَعَانِ	تَنْصُرَانِ	تَضْرِبَانِ
Plural	تَفْتَحْنَ	تَكْرُمْنَ	تَحْسِبْنَ	تَسْمَعْنَ	تَنْصُرْنَ	تَضْرِبْنَ

متكلم مذكر و مؤنث

1st Per.mas./fem.

Sing.	اَفْتَحُ	اَكْرُمُ	اَحْسِبُ	اَسْمَعُ	اَنْصُرُ	اَضْرِبُ
Plural	نَفْتَحُ	نَكْرُمُ	نَحْسِبُ	نَسْمَعُ	نَنْصُرُ	نَضْرِبُ

VOCABULARY

sara	**سار ؛ يسير**	naba'a	**نبعَ**
to go, to be in motion		*to spring, originate*	
sair	**سير**	mamba'	**منبع – منابع**
walk, march		*source, origin*	
sahra	**صحراء**	karaqa	**خرق**
desert		*to penetrate*	
'ajjala	**عجل : استعجل**	kariq	**خارق العادة**
to hasten		*extraordinary*	
'ajala	**عجل : سرعة**	faza	**فاز ؛ يفوز**
haste, speed		*to triumph*	

nadima ندم ؛ يندم

to repent

nādim نادم

repentant

d̲i'b ذئب

wolf, jackal

kafara كفر ؛ يكفر

to deny, to be ungrateful

ḥaḍāra حضارة

civilization, culture

faḍīla فضيلة

excellent quality, virtue

karāma كرامة

dignity, respect

rabī' ربيع

spring season

ṣaif صيف

summer

k̲arīf خريف

autumn

shitā شتاء

winter

id̲ā'a إذاعة

broadcast

fauz فوز : ظفر : نجاح

success, victory

fāiz فائز : ناجح : فاتح

winner

tamattu' تمتع

enjoyment

waraq ورق : قرطاس

paper

t̲allāja ثلاجة : مثلج

refrigerator, ice-cold

safīna سفينة

boat, ship

afsada أفسد ؛ يفسد

to spoil, to corrupt

fasād فساد

corruption, wickedness

waḥasha وحشة

loneliness, desolation

ṣabba صب ؛ يصب

to pour, fill

jiha جهة - جهات

side, direction

at̲ar أثر - آثار

impression, monument

rādiyo راديو
radio
musā'ada مساعدة
assistance, help, aid
naṣara نصر ؛ ينصر
to help
ṣalā صلوة
prayer
shahr شهر – اشهر
month
qādim قادم : مقبل
arriving, next
ash-shahr alqādim الشهر القادم
the next month
qufl قفل
lock, bolt
miftāḥ مفتاح
key
maftūḥ مفتوح
opened, open
'ātifi عاطفي
emotional, sentimental
ragman 'an رغما عن
in spite of

dam دم – دماء
blood
tasbiḥ تسبيح : حمد
praise of God
qaddasa قدس ؛ يقدس
to sanctify, to glorify
muqaddis مقدس : متقدس
holy, reverent
ulūhiya ألوهية
divinity
ihāna إهانة : إزدراء
contempt, insult
'adāla ijtimā'iya عدالة إجتماعية
social justice
qāfila قافلة
caravan
farrāsh فراش
office boy
ishtadda إشتد
to grow severe, violent
tahāni تهاني : مبرزك
congratulations, felicitation
ta'aziya تعزية
condolence, solace

Observe the use of the verb in the Imperfect tense in the following sentences.

TRANSLATION	*MODEL SENTENCES*
1. The boys are playing with the ball.	١- يلعب الأولاد بالكرة.
2. Fish live in water.	٢- يعيش السمك في الماء.
3. Rain falls from the sky.	٣- ينزل المطر من السماء.
4. The sun rises from the east.	٤- تطلع الشمس من المشرق.
5. Mahmood is purchasing a pen.	٥- يشتري محمود القلم.
6. The boat is floating on the water.	٦- تجري السفينة في الماء
7. We will take a walk (for recreation) in the garden.	٧- سوف نتنزه في الحدائق
8. The boy will swim in the river.	٨- سوف يسبح الغلام في النهر
9. The leaves of the trees fall in autumn.	٩- تسقط أوراق الأشجار في الخريف.
10. Heat becomes severe in summer.	١٠-يشتد الحر في الصيف.
11. The merchant is selling the furniture.	١١-يبيع التاجر الأثاث.
12. The child is crying in the cradle.	١٢-يصرخ الطفل في المهد.
13. A trade delegation from Iraq will reach New Delhi tomorrow.	١٣-يصل إلى دلهي الجديدة غدا وفد تجاري من العراق.
14. His Excellency the Ambassador of the Kingdom of Saudi Arabia will visit Madras next month.	١٤-سيزور سيادة سفير المملكة العربية السعودية مدراس في الشهر القادم.
15. I am sending my regards to you.	١٥-أبلغ سلامي إليك

16. I will spend the spring in the south.	١٦-أقضي الربيع في الجنوب.
17. Caravan(s) pass in the desert of Arabia.	١٧-تسير القوافل بصحراء العرب.
18. One who hastes will repent.	١٨-من يستعجل يندم.
19. Children are afraid of the wolf.	١٩-يخاف الأطفال من الذئب.
20. Fowzia understands her lesson.	٢٠-تفهم فوزية درسها.
21. The peasant cultivates wheat.	٢١-يزرع الفلاح القمح.
22. The wind enters the room.	٢٢-يدخل الهواء في الحجرة.
23. The girl is cleaning the clothes.	٢٣-تنظف البنت الثياب.
24. The woman cooked the food.	٢٤-طبخت المرأة الطعام.
25. The girl milked the cow.	٢٥-حلبت الفتاة البقرة.
26. Snow falls in winter.	٢٦-يسقط الثلج شتاء.
27. You will hear an important announcement on the radio.	٢٧-سوف تسمعون إعلانا هاما من المذياع (راديو).
28. I am seeking your help.	٢٨-أطلب مساعدتك.
29. We ask for God's help.	٢٩-نستعين بالله.
30. We start our day with a prayer.	٣٠ نفتتح يومنا بالصلوة.

LESSON SEVENTEEN

The Imperative and the Negative Command

WOMEN'S EDUCATION

تعليم المـــرأة

1. A discussion took place in the municipal council regarding the advancement of women. A speaker told the person who opposes this concept "Women in former times were not offered all the opportunities which were available for men. They were not given educational facilities until recently."

١-جرت المناقشة في مجلس البلديـــة حول نهضة المرأة - وقال متحدث لشخص يعارض هذه الفكـــرة: "إن المرأة في عصور التاريخ لم تتـــح لها كل الفرص التي اتيحت للرجال ولم تتح لها سبل التعليم إلا مـــن عهد قريب".

2. Open your minds and eyes and look at the reality of the world around you. Send your daughter to school for training and education and treat her as you would treat your sons and defend her rights.

٢-"إفتح ذهنك وعينك وانظر إلـــى حقيقة العالم حولك - أرسل إبنتـك الي المدرسة للتربيـــة والتعليـــم وعاملها كما تعامل إبنك ودافع عن حقوقهـــا".

3. Bestow your complete love on her and give her whatever she needs.

٣-وامنحها حبك الكامل واعطها مـــا تحتاج إليه".

4. And he added saying "Co-operate with women in the reformation of society and solution of its problems and trust her in general matters."

٤-وأضاف قائلا: "تعاونوا مع المـــرأة في اصلاح المجتمع وحل مشـــاكله واعتمدوا عليـــها فـــي الشـــئون العامة.

5. "Make use of her services for every position which suits her nature. Let each of us do his duty in this cause so that we may take her out from darkness into light."

واستخدموها في كل منصب يناسبها طبيعيا". ليعمل كل منا واجبه في هذا السبيل حتى نخرجها من الظلمات إلى النور.

The Imperatives:

The Imperative, فعل الأمر is formed from المضارع المخاطب *Imperfect 2nd person*. Rules for making the Imperative are as follows:

1. If the letter after the sign of مُضَارِع is with the vowel sign, drop the sign of مُضَارِع and add ـْ to the last letter. e.g.

تَعِدُ - عِدْ	تَزِنُ - زِنْ	تَضَعُ - ضَعْ
Promise!	*Weigh!*	*Put!*

2. If the letter, after the sign of مُضَارِع is without the vowel sign, add "hamza" ا in the beginning after dropping the sign of مُضَارِع and add ـْ to the last letter.

(a) Then look at the vowel of the 2nd radical, if it is ـُ add the same to ا "the hamzat al wasal". e.g.

تَنْصُرُ - اُنْصُرْ	تَنْظُرُ - اُنْظُرْ	تَقْرُبُ - اُقْرُبْ
help!	*look!*	*come near!*

(b) But if the second radical has ـِ or ـَ as its vowel, then give ـِ to ا "the hamzat al wasal": e.g.

تَصْرِفُ - إِصْرِفْ	تَضْرِبُ - إِضْرِبْ	تَحْسِبُ - إِحْسِبْ
spend!	*strike!*	*suppose!*
تَشْرَبُ - إِشْرَبْ	تَسْمَعُ - إِسْمَعْ	تَذْهَبُ - إِذْهَبْ
drink!	*hear!*	*go!*

(3) Further, after adopting the above procedure, if any of the "weak letters", ا , و , ي are found at the end, they are dropped, so is ن which is used as a vowel.

The Negative Command:

The positive command is changed into a negative command by prefixing لا to المضارع المخاطب *Imperfect 2nd person,* further the last letter is made vowel-less. e.g.

Do not grieve لا تحْزَنْ ← تحزَنْ *Do not fear* لا تَخَفْ ← تَخاف

Conjugation of the Imperative and Negative command.

فِعْـلُ الأمرُ والـنَّهْيُ

2nd person Mas.

لاتَفْعَلْ	أُدْعُ	إحْسِبْ	أُنْصُرْ	عِـدْ	إفْعَلْ	Sing.
لاتَفْعَلا	أُدْعُوَا	إحْسِبَا	أُنْصُرَا	عِـدا	إفْعَلا	Dual
لاتَفْعَلُوْا	أُدْعُوا	إحْسِبُوا	أُنْصُرُوْا	عِـدُوا	إفْعَلُوا	Plural

2nd person Fem.

لاتَفْعَلِي	أُدْعِي	إحْسِبِي	أُنْصُرِي	عِـدِي	إفْعَلِي	Sing.
لاتَفْعَلا	أُدْعُوَا	إحْسِبَا	أُنْصُرَا	عِـدا	إفْعَلا	Dual
لاتَفْعَلْنَ	أُدْعِينَ	إحْسِبْنَ	أُنْصُرْنَ	عِـدْنَ	إفْعَلْنَ	Plural

---

إفعلْ* do لا تفعلْ** don't do

VOCABULARY

amr أمر - أوامر
command, authority

taḥta amrika تحت أمرك
at your service, disposal

amara أمر ؛يأمر
to order, instruct

naha نهى ؛ ينهى
to prohibit, forbid

sabīl سبيل
way, possibility

dihn ذهن - أذهان
mind, intellect

ḥaqīqa حقيقة - حقائق
fact, reality

ḥaqq حق - حقوق
one's due, property

kada'a خدع : ختل
to deceive, cheat

mutakabbir متكبر : فخور
proud, boasting

fakara فخر
to be proud

iqra' إقرأ
read

qara' قرأ ؛ يقرأ
to read

'azama 'ala عزم على
to resolve upon, to determine

baladiya بلديـــة
municipality, township

furṣa فرصة - فرص
opportunity, chance

manaḥa منح ؛ يمنح
to grant, award

ẓulm ظلم
injustice, oppression

ẓalama ظلم ؛ يظلم
to oppress

ẓālim ظالم
unjust, tyrant

maẓlūm مظلوم
innocent, oppressed

aqāma أقام ؛ يقيم
to establish, to reside

mu'ārada معارضة
opposition, protest
'aṣri عصري
modern, contemporary
'asa عسى : لعل
may be, perhaps
ma'rūf معروف : إحسان
known, accepted, good
aḥsana أحسن
to do well, to do right
munkar منكر
an abomination, forbidden
mu'āmala معاملة
social life, transaction
manzil منزل : مثوى
dwelling place, house
manṣib منصب - مناصب
position, rank, post
munāsib مناسب
suitable, fitting
ḍa'īf ضعيف - ضعفاء
weak
qawiy قوي - أقوياء
strong, vigorous

iqāma إقامة
residence, residence permit
ṣaut صوت - أصوات
vote, noise, voice, sound
ṣabara صبر ؛ يصبر
to be patient
ṣidq صدق : حق : حقيقة
truth, right
muṣība مصيبة
misfortune, calamity
tajassasa تجسس
to spy, to explore
jāsus جاسوس - جواسيس
spy
ba'ḍ بعض
some, part
ba'ḍukum ba'ḍan بعضكم بعضا
each other
bug̱ḍ بغض
hatred
isti'mār إستعمار
colonialism
tad̲akkara تذكر
to keep in mind, to think of

taraka ترك ؛ يترك
to leave, to quit

ṣunbur صنبور : حنفية
tap

rama رمى ؛ يرمي
to throw

rahīb رهيب : مخيف
fearful

istaiqaẓa إستيقظ
to wake up

iḥtarama إحترم ؛ يحترم
to respect

ḥafiẓa حفظ ؛ يحفظ
to memorize, to protect

iṣlāh إصلاح
repair, reformation

mu'min مؤمن
believer, faithful

sallama سلم على : حيا
to salute, greet

tabḏīr تبذير : إسراف
squandering, waste

mā'āẓam ما أعظم
how great!

taḏkira تذكرة : مذكرة
ticket, note

taṭawwur تطور
development, progress

naṭaqa نطق ؛ ينطق
to utter, to speak

ihmāl إهمال : تهامل
negligence

ahmala أهمل ؛ يهمل
to neglect

ishāra-tul-murūr إشارة المرور
traffic signal

miskīn مسكين
needy, poor

ibn as-sabīl إبن السبيل
wayfarer

lubāb لباب
marrow, best part

sharīr شرير : ردي : فاسد
wicked, bad, decayed

qishr قشر
peal, crust

mā ajmal ما أجمل
how beautiful!

Observe the use of the verb in the imperative and negative forms in the following sentences:

TRANSLATION	*MODEL SENTENCES*
1. Be kind towards the orphans, the disabled and the wayfarer.	١-إرحَم اليتامى والمساكين وابن السبيل.
2. Let not people ridicule others, who perhaps may be better than themselves.	٢-لا يسخَر قوم من قوم عسى أن يكونوا خيرًا منهم.
3. Do not call those who are slain in the way of God as dead. But they are living.	٣-ولا تقولوا لِمَن يُقتل في سبيل الله أموات بل أحياء.
4. God said to Moses and Aron, "Go, both of you, to Pharoah, certainly he has transgressed (the bounds)".	٤-قال الله لموسى وهٰرون إذهَبا إلى فرعون إنه طغى.
5. Remember (all of you) the favor of God upon you.	٥-أذكروا نعمَةَ الله عليكم.
6. O those who believe! Do not enter houses other than your own, until you have asked permission, and salute the inmates therein. That is best for you, that perhaps you may be heedful!	٦-يا أيها الذين آمنوا لا تدخلوا بُيوتا غير بيوتكم حتى تستأنِسُوا وتسلموا على أهلها ذلكم خير لكم لعلكم تذكرون.
7. Respect the guests and make their stay comfortable.	٧-أكرموا الضيوف وأحسنوا مثواهم.
8. Sabiha, clean the dining table, arrange the reception room and cook food for us.	٨-يا صبيحة! نظّفِي المائدة، رتّبي حجرة الجلوس واطبخي لنا الطعام

9. Write your lesson, Zainab.	٩- أكتبِي درسك يا زينب.
10. Do not go to your work late.	١٠- لا تذهب إلي عملك متأخرا.
11. Feed the poor.	١١- أطعِم الفقراء.
12. Do not spy nor backbite each other.	١٢- لا تجسسوا ولا يَغتب بعضكم بعضا.
13. Do not put off today's work for tomorrow.	١٣- لا تؤخِّر عمل اليوم إلي غد
14. Walk on the road on the left side, stop if you see red light on the traffic signal. And help the blind and the weak in crossing the road.	١٤- سِر في الشارع علي الجانب الأيسر قِف إذا رأيت النور الأحمر في إشارة المـُرور وساعد العَمي والضعَفاء علي عبور الشارع.
15. Listen to thc advice of the doctor.	١٥- إسمع نصيحة الطبيب.
16. O my brother! Do not leave the water tap open. Do not write on the wall of the house nor throw the waste paper and peel of the fruits except in the waste-paper basket.	١٦- يا أخي لا تترك صُنبور الماء مفتوحا ولا تكتب علي حائط البيت ولا ترم الورق المهمل وقشر الفوَاكِه إلا في سلة المُهملات.
17. Go to sleep early and wake up early.	١٧- نِم مبكرا واستيقظ مبكرا.
18. Respect the teacher.	١٨- إحترِم المعلم / أستاذ
19. Memorise your lesson.	١٩- إحفَظ درسك.
20. Speak the truth.	٢٠- إنطِق بالصدق.

LESSON EIGHTEEN

Active and Passive Voice — المعلوم والمجهول

Transitive and Intransitive — الفعل المتعدي واللازم

GARDENS OF RIYADH — حدائق الرياض

1. Riyadh is a beautiful city. Its weather is warm and its air is dry. Its roads are wide and its buildings are lofty. It has well-arranged gardens.

١- الرِّيَاض مَدِينَة جَمِيلَة وجَوُّهَا دَافِئ. وهَوَاها جَاف. وشَوَارِعُها واسِعَة ومَبَانِيهَا شَامِخَة وفِيهَا حَدائِق مُنسقَة.

2. Public gardens exist in all parts of the city and its vicinity. Green grass is grown and comfortable seats are placed under the trees.

٢- تَنشأ الحَدائِق العَامَّة في جَمِيع أنْحَاءِ المَدِينَة وضوَاحِيهَا ويُزْرَع الحَشِيشُ الأخْضَر فِي أرضِهَا وتُوضَع مَقَاعِد مُريحَة فِي ظِلِّ الشَّجَر.

3. The inhabitants of the city love these gardens and enjoy the city's delightful sights.

٣- وسُكَّان المَدِينَة يُحِبُّون هذِه الحَدائِق ويَتَمَتَّعُون بِمنَاظِرِهَا الرَّائِعَة.

4. Some boys were seen picking flowers. That spoils the beauty of the garden.

٤- ويُرَى بَعضَ الأولاد يَقطِفُون الأزهَار وذلِك يُفسِد بَهْجَة الحَدِيقة.

5. Do not touch the flowers in public gardens nor walk on the grass.

٥- لا تَلمَس أزْهَارَ الْحَدَائِق العَامَّة وَلا تَمْشِ عَلَى الْحَشِيْش.

Active and Passive Voice المعلوم والمجهول

The verb in the active voice is called by the Arab Grammarians الفعل المعلوم فاعله *the action, of which the agent is known.* The verb in the passive voice is called الفعل المجهول فاعله *the action, of which the agent is unknown.*

Passive المجهول	Active المعلوم
زُرِعَ القُطْنُ	زَرَعَ الفلاّح القُطْنَ
Cotton was cultivated.	*The peasant cultivated cotton.*
كُسِرَتْ الزُّجَاجَةُ	كَسَرَ الوَلَدُ الزُّجَاجَةَ
The glass has been broken.	*The boy has broken the glass.*
يُصْنَعُ الكُرْسِيُّ	يَصْنَعُ النَّجَّارُ الكُرْسِيَّ
The chair is being made.	*The carpenter is making the chair.*

The sentences on the right consist of a verb, a subject and an object. When compared with the sentences opposite to these, two major changes in the construction of these sentences are found:

1. The verbs have been converted into the passive voice.
2. The Subject of the "active voice" is an "agent", whose act affects an object. The subject of the "passive voice" is the object of sentences in the first group; so it is called in Arabic نائب الفاعل.
3. Further the verbs in the second group agree with the gender of نائب الفاعل *"Subject of the passive".*

The passive is not used in Arabic when the "agent" of the act is mentioned. A passive sentence in English such as: "A letter was written by Zaki" when translated into Arabic would read كتب ذكي الرسالة *Zaki wrote the letter.*

The passive is formed from the active by a change of vowels.

In the past perfect, الماضي the first radical takes ُ the second radical takes ِ and the third radical remains unchanged.

Passive	**المجهول**	**Active**	**المعلوم**
he was beaten	ضُرِبَ	*he beat*	ضَرَبَ
he was heard	سُمِعَ	*he heard*	سَمِعَ
he was helped	نُصِرَ	*he helped*	نَصَرَ

In the Imperfect Tense, المُضَارِع the prefix (sign of the Imperfect) takes ُ, the second radical takes َ and the last vowel remains unchanged.

Passive	**المجهول**	**Active**	**المعلوم**
he is being beaten	يُضْرَبُ	*he is beating*	يَضْرِبُ
he is being heard	يُسْمَعُ	*he is hearing*	يَسْمَعُ
he is being helped	يُنْصَرُ	*he is helping*	يَنْصُرُ

Transitive And Intransitive المُتعدِّي واللاَّزم

A discussion on the Active and Passive voice leads to the division of verbs into المُتَعَدِّي *The Transitive* and اللاَّزِمْ *The Intransitive.*

A transitive verb, مُتَعَدِّي is a verb with an object. In the sentence كَتَبَ التِّلمِيذُ مَقالة *the student wrote an essay,* كتب is a Transitive verb. Other examples of such verbs are:

زَرَعَ	رَكِبَ	كَسَرَ	ضَرَبَ	جَرَّ
to cultivate	*to ride*	*to break*	*to strike*	*to pull*

A verb, which expresses a state or condition or signifies an act which is confined to the subject, is an Intransitive verb, **لازم.** In the sentence **جَلَسَ الْوَلَدُ عَلَى الكُرْسِـــي** *the boy sat on the chair,* **جَلَسَ** is an intransitive verb. Some more examples of such verbs are:

ذَهَبَ	جَاءَ	بَكَى	مَرِضَ	نَـــامَ
to go	*to come*	*to weep*	*to be sick*	*to sleep*

Note: Only transitive verbs can be used in the passive voice.

The verbs with the pattern of كَـــرُمَ *to be generous,* are all intransitive.

VOCABULARY

jawāz as-safar	جواز السفر	ṣūf	صوف
passport		*wool*	
tashīra	تأشيرة	quṭn	قطن
visa		*cotton*	
ḥajz	حجز	ḥarīr	حرير
reservation		*silk*	
mutamassik	متمسك	tabarr'a	تبرع
holding fast, clinging		*to contribute, donate*	
zāra	زار	armala	أرملة
to visit		*widow*	
zāir	زائر	yatīm	يتيم – يتامى
visitor		*orphan*	
ziyāra	زيارة	ta'mīn	تأمين
visit		*insurance*	

ḵashab خشب

wood, timber

ḥaṭab حطب

firewood

qitāl قتال : صراع

battle, struggle

jabhat alqitāl جبهة القتال

war front

ishtirākiya إشتراكية

socialism

rasmāliya رأسمالية

capitalism

'aamm عام : شامل

general, comprehensive

al amn al 'aamm الأمن العام

public security

arrai al-'aamm الرأي العام

public opinion

qanūn قانون : نظام

law, code, regulation

naẓama نظم : إنتظم : رتب

to organize, arrange

niẓām نظام : ترتيب

arrangement, system

tamatta'a تمتع : استمتع

to enjoy

shamma شم : اشتم

to smell

raunaq رونق : بهجة

splendor

jawād جواد : سخي

generous, liberal

baḵīl بخيل

miser, greedy

binaya بناية : عمارة

building

qabaḍa قبض ؛ يقبض

to hold, arrest

qabḍ قبض : مسك

constipation, grasping

qabr قبر

grave

tawḏīb توضيب

processing, preparation

taṭawwur تطور

development, evolution

qamūs قاموس – قواميس

dictionary

‘azīm	عظيم : باهر	a’alana	أعلن ؛ يعلن
splendid, magnificent		*to declare, announce*	
surūr	سرور : مسرة : فرح	ẓill	ظل
delight		*shadow, shade*	
musābaqa	مسابقة الخطابية	qiṭ’a	قطعة
competition,contest		*part, piece*	
‘aṣabi	عصبي	massa	مس ؛ يمس
nervous		*to touch*	
mustalzamāt	مستلزمات	ikṯilās	إختلاس
requirements		*misappropriation*	
ḡubār	غبار : تراب	ḡarasa	غرس ؛ يغرس
dust		*to plant trees*	
asliḥa	أسلحة	injāz	إنجاز : تنجيز
weapon, arms		*completion, accomplishment*	
I’tirāf	إعتراف	ittifāq	إتفاق
recognition, confession		*agreement, treaty*	
Iltizām	إلتزام	muwāfaqa	موافقة
necessity, commitment		*approval, conformity*	

Observe the use of the verbs in the active and passive voice, in the following sentences:

TRANSLATION	***MODEL SENTENCES***
1. Clothes are woven from wool or cotton or silk.	١ – تُنسَج الثياب من الصوف أو القطن أو الحرير.

2. Donation is collected for the poor, the disabled and the orphans.	٢- تُجْمَعُ التَّبَرُّعات لِمُساعدَة الفُقَــراء والمَسَاكِين واليَتَامَى.
3. Leather was exported to foreign countries.	٣- صُدِرَت الجُلُود إلى الخَارِج.
4. Prizes have been distributed to the winners of the match.	٤- قد قُسِمَت الجَوَائِز للفائِــزين فِــي المَبَارات.
5. The rocket has been fired.	٥-قــد أطلِق الصَّارُوخ.
6. The house was constructed with speed.	٦-شُيِدَ البِنَاء بِسُرعَةٍ.
7. The professor gave a lecture.	٧-ألقى الأستَاذ مُحاضَرَة.
8. Money has been stolen.	٨-قد سُرِق المَــال.
9. The results of the annual examination were announced.	٩-أعلِنَت نتَائِج الإمتِحَانات السَّنَوية.
10. Ibn Khaldun was born in Tunis and taught at Cairo.	١٠-وُلِد ابنُ خَلدُون فِي تُونس وكــانَ يُدرس في القاهِرة.
11. The child slept in the cradle.	١١-نام الطفلُ في المَهْــد.
12. The visitor sat on the chair.	١٢-جلسَ الزائِــر على الكُرسِيِّ.
13. The student went out of his house.	١٣-خَرجَ التِّلميذ مِن بَيتِه.
14. The girl became happy with the reward.	١٤-فرحت البِنتُ بالجَــائِزة
15. The chair is made of wood.	١٥-يُصنع الكُرسِي من الخَشَبِ.
16. The soldier was killed on the war front.	١٦-قد قُتِلَ الجُندِيُّ علَى جَبهَةِالقِــتَال.

17. The camel carried the firewood.	١٧-حَملَ الجَمَلُ الحَطبَ.
18. The firewood has been carried.	١٨-قــد حُمِل الحَطبُ.
19. The government develops public gardens.	١٩-تنَشى الحُكُومةُ الحَدائِق العَامـــة.
20. Public gardens are being developed.	٢٠-تُنْشَـــأ الحدَائِـــق العَـــامَّةُ.
21. The gardener is planting the tree.	٢١-يَغْرِسُ البُسْتَاني الشَّجر.
22. The tree is being planted.	٢٢-يُغْرَس الشجَـــرُ.
23. Thc engineer lays the streets.	٢٣-يُنظِّمُ المُهندِس الطُرق.
24. The streets are being laid.	٢٤-تُنَظَّم الطُرق.
25. Grapes have been cultivated in the school garden.	٢٥-زُرِع العِنبُ في حدِيثة المدرَسَة.
26. I was happy about the success of my friend in the oral contest.	٢٦-سُرِرتُ بِنجَــاح صديِقِـــي فــــي مسابقـــة الخِطابة.
27. The wind blew.	٢٧-هَبَّــتِ الرِّيح.

LESSON NINETEEN

Moods of the Imperfect Tense

المضارع المنصوب والمضارع المجزوم

INDUSTRIAL CENTER

مركز الصناعة

1. Usman wanted to visit the industrial center in Helwaan. He suggested this to his father and requested that he accompany him to Helwaan.

١- أرَاد عُثمَان أن يزُورَ المَركَز الصّنَاعَي في حَلوَان فَعَرَضَ هذِه الفِكرَة عَلي وَالدِه وطَلبَ مِنه أن يصْحبَه إلي حَلوَان؟

2. The father asked: “Why do you wish to visit that area?”

٢- قال الوَالِد: "لماذا تُحِب أن تزُور تلك المَنطقة؟"

3. Usman replied “I wish to see the iron and steel factory there and the other factories so that my knowledge expands and I have a clear picture of our progress in the industrial field.”

٣- قالَ عُثمَان: "أحِب أن أشَاهِد فِيها مَصنَع الحدِيد والصُّلب والمَصَانِع الأخرَى أيضًا كَي تَنمُو مَعلُومَاتِي ولأعرفَ صُورَة واضِحَة عَن تقدُّمِنا في مَيدَان الصِّنَاعَة.

4. The father was happy with Usman’s reply and he told him: “I will accompany you, Usman, but it is necessary that you write down what appeals to you”.

٤- سرَّ الوَالِد مِن إجَابَةِ عُثمَان وقال له: "سَأصَاحِبُكَ يَا عُثمَان ولكِن عَليكَ أنْ تَكتُبَ كُلَّ مَا يُعجِبُك".

Introduction

The Imperfect tense. الفعل المضارع, conveys the meaning of the present and the future tense. But due to the addition of certain particles before it, the meaning of مضارع undergoes a change, and sometimes change occurs not only in the meaning but also in the word. As mentioned earlier, the addition of سوف and س before مضارع converts it into the future tense.

Changes in the Meaning of Imperfect

The Imperfect المضارع has five "moods", which are identified by the vowel of the third radical. In this respect it resembles the noun الإسم with its three case-endings.

The simplest use of a verb is to make a statement of fact, or ask a question. But a verb may also be used to express a command, or to express a mere supposition or a wish. These different manners in which a verb may be used to express an action are called "moods".

The Imperfect المضــارع has five "moods"; namely, the Indicative, Subjunctive, Jussive or Conditional, Imperative and Energetic.

The Indicative and Imperative "moods" have been dealt with in lessons 16 and 17 respectively.

PARTICLES WHICH CHANGE THE MEANING OF THE IMPERFECT

There are three groups of particles which place either ـَ or ـْ or "the ن of emphasis" at the end of the imperfect. With this addition it is called (1) المضارع المنصـوب *the Subjunctive* (2) المضارع المجزوم *the Jussive* and (3) المضارع مــع نــون التــأكيد *the Energetic of the Imperfect.* But in the absence of any of these particles normal الفعل المضارع *the Imperfect* will end with "Damma" ـُ.

THE SUBJUNCTIVE المَضارِع المَنْصُوب

The particles which add ـَ to the مُضَارِع are:

(1) أن *that* (2) لَن *certainly not* (3) إذَنْ *in that case*

(4) كَيْ *in order that* e.g.

كَيْ يَـذْهَبَ	لَنْ يَذْهَبَ	أنْ يَذْهَبَ
that he goes	*he will never go*	*in order that he goes*

THE JUSSIVE المَضارِع المَجزُوم

The particles which add ـْ to the مُضَارِع are: (1) لَمْ *not* (2) لام الأمر *the* ل *of command,* (3) لا النهي *the* لا *of prohibition.* (it expresses the prohibition of an act or a wish that something is not to be done) (4) إن *if* and (5) لَمَّا *never.* e.g.

1. لَمْ يَفْعَلْ	2. لِيُنْفِقْ ذُو سَعَةٍ	3. لاَ تَحْزَنْ
He did not do	*The prosperous shall spend*	*Do not grieve*

THE ENERGETIC OF THE IMPERFECT المُضَارِع معَ النُّون التَّأكيـد

"The ن of emphasis" comes at the end of مُضارِع, after "ل *with fatha*" is prefixed to it e.g.

لِيَفْعَـلَنَّ *he will certainly do* لَيَنْصُرَنَّ الله *certainly God will help*

The "Energetic" forms of the Imperfect المُضارِع have always a future connotation. e.g.

لَئِنْ اَنْجَيْتَنا مِنْ هَذِهِ لَنَكُونَـنَّ مِـنَ الشَّاكِرِيْـنَ *If you deliver us from this (danger), certainly we will be (from the) thankful.*

VOCABULARY

min faḍlak من فضلك : تفضل

Please

rajā̄ رجاء : أمل

hope, request

amāna امانة

reliability, trust

ṣarafa صرف ؛ يصرف

to spend, to change money

maṣrif مصرف : بنك

bank

ista'dda إستعد

to get ready

takṯīṭ تخطيط

planning

tansīq تنسيق

systematic arrangement

baṭṭāl بطــال

unemployed

waẓif وظيفة : خدمة

job, employment

alqā ألقى ؛ يلقي

to throw, deliver

saḥaba سحب ؛ يسحب

to withdraw, to pull

arāda أراد ؛ يريد

to wish, to desire

irāda إرادة : مشية

will, choice

waqafa وقف ؛ يقف

to stand

auqafa أوقف : منع

to prevent, to stop

mauqif موقف

attitude, position

waqf وقف - أوقاف

endowment

marra مر ؛ يمر

to pass by, proceed

ḥarakat al murūr حركة المرور

the traffic

man' tajawwul منع التجول

curfew

ḍagaṭa ضغط

to press

alqa bayanān ʻan ألقى بيانا عن

to make a statement about

jamʿiya taawuhiyya جمعية تعاونية

co-operative society

ḍamān ضمان : ضمانة

surety, guarantee

taḍāmun تضامن

solidarity

maḍmūn مضمون

guaranteed, insured

miʿṭaf معطف

overcoat

rāfaqa رافق

to accompany

murfaq bihi مرفق به

enclosed, attached

ihtamma إهتم ؛ يهتم

to pay attention

ṣarāha صراحة

frankness

wāḍih واضح

clear, evident, obvious

adda أدى

to discharge, carry out

ḍaḡṭ ad-dam ضغط الدم

blood pressure

ittiḥād إتحاد : وفاق

unity, union

niqāba نقابة

trade union, guild

raqāba رقابة

censorship

kallama كلم ؛ يكلم

to speak

sitār ستـار

curtain, veil

minṭaqa منطقة

zone, area

nashara نشر ؛ ينشر

to spread, unfold

kibrīt كبريت

sulphur, matches

mindīl منديل

kerchief

duḵān دخان

smoke

mustawa alḥaya مستوى الحياة

standard of living

shahr al 'asal	شهر العسل	mallāḥ	ملاح
honeymoon		*sailor, mariner*	
'asl	عسل	mallāḥa	ملاحة
honey		*navigation, shipping*	
shaqqa	شقة	shabi'a	شبع ؛ يشبع
flat, apartment		*to satisfy one's appetite*	
ṭābaq	طابق	shab'ān	شبعان
floor, story		*satisfied, sated*	
fikra	فكرة : أفكار	mudhish	مدهش
thought, idea		*amazing, marvelous*	

Observe the use of the Imperfect tense in different forms, in the following sentences.

TRANSLATION	***MODEL SENTENCES***
1. I wish to visit Arab countries.	١- أريد أن أزور البلدان العربية.
2. I like to play football.	٢- أحب أن ألعب كرة القدم.
3. The policeman stood to regulate traffic.	٣- وقف الشرطي كي ينظم المرور.
4. I purchased a ticket so that I may watch the hockey match.	٤- إشتريت تذكرة كي أشاهد مباراة "هاكي".
5. Man toils in his young age that he could relax in old age.	٥- يتعب المرأ في صغره كي يستريح في كبره.
6. The student prepared to deliver a speech in the meeting (gathering).	٦- إستعد التلميذ ليلقي كلمة في الحفلة.

7. The officer will never delay his work.	٧- لنْ يتأخرَ الموظف عن عمله.
8. The lazy person never succeeds.	٨- لنْ يفوزَ الكسلان.
9. Work with sincerity that you may receive great reward from God.	٩- إعمل بـــاخلاص حتـــى تنـــالَ الجزاء العظيم من الله.
10. It pleases me to offer my thanks to all those who have attended the party.	١٠- يسرني أن أقدمَ شكري لكل مـــن إشترك في الحفلة.
11. The father instructed his son to brush his teeth before and after sleep.	١١- أمر الوالد إبنه أن يغسلَ أسنانه قبل النوم وبعده.
12. Be polite, so that you could be acceptable (popular).	١٢- كُنْ مؤدبا كي تكونَ محبوبا.
13. I went to Basrah in order to learn the Arabic language.	١٣- ذهبت إلي البصرة كـــي أتعلـــمَ اللغة العربيـــة.
14. I acquire knowledge in order to serve my country and my people.	١٤- أتعلم كي أخدمَ وطني وأهلي.
15. The state pays attention to the development of industry so that the standard of living may rise.	١٥- تهتم الدولة بنشـــر الصناعـــة ليرقيَ مستوى المعيشة.
16. The sailor raises the sail of the boat so that the wind may push it.	١٦- ينشر الملاح شـــراع الســـفينة ليدفعها الهواء.
17. I will never eat when I am satisfied (saturated).	١٧- لن آكلَ وأنا شبعـــان.

18. The peasant will never sell his land.

١٨- لنْ يبيعَ الفلاح أرضَه.

19. The student said to his teacher, "I have completed my homework". The teacher replied to him, "In that case you will succeed".

١٩- قال التلميذ لأستاذه: "لقد أديت واجبي" فأجاب الأستاذ: "إذن تنجحَ".

20. Do not grieve; certainly God is with you!

٢٠- لا تحزنْ إن الله معك.

21. You shall not attain righteousness unless you give (in charity) that which you love.

٢١- لنْ تنالُوا البرَّ حتَّى تنفقوا مما تُحِبُّون.

22. It is essential that you ponder over a work before you start it.

٢٢- يجب أن تُفكِّرَ فِي العمل قبل الشروع فِيه.

23. The girl said to her mother: "I will be diligent in my studies". She responded: "In that case you shall get distinction".

٢٣- قالت البنت لأمها: "سأجتهدَ في الدراسةَ". فأجابت الأم: "إذنْ تبلغي المجد".

LESSON TWENTY

كَانَ and its Categories كان وأخَواتُها

The Verbs of Incomplete Predication

FAISAL — فيصل

1. Faisal is a sportsman. He learnt swimming and became strong in mind and body.

١- فيصَل شَابٌ رياضِي تَعلَّمَ السبَّاحَة فاصبْحَ قويا صَحِيح الْجِسمِ والْعقْل.

2. One day Faisal woke up early in the morning. He was walking on the bank of a river which was near his village. He was extremely happy as the weather became clear and the sun was not warm.

٢- وفِي يَوم مِنَ الأيَّام استَيْقظ فيصَل مُبكِّرًا وكانَ يَمشِي علَى شَاطئ نَهْر قريب مِن قريتِهِ وكَان فِي غايَة السُّرُور حَيثُ صار الْجَو صَحْواً ولَيستِ الشَّمسُ مُحرقة.

3. As Faisal was walking on the river bank, he saw a boy about to be drowned in the river. He rushed towards him. He rescued him and rendered him first-aid. He removed water from his abdomen and remained by his side till the boy recovered consciousness. He advised him: "Do not get into the river so long as the current is strong".

٣- وبَينمَا فيصَل يَسِيرُ علَى شَاطئ إذْ رأى صَبيا يكَادُ يغْرق فِي النَّهْر فهرْوَلَ إليهِ وأنْقذه وَأسْعَفه وأخْرَجَ الْمَاء مِنْ بَطْنِه ومَازالَ فيصَل إلي جَنبهِ حَتى أفاقَ الصَّبي من إغْمَاء وقَال لَه لاتَنزل النَّهرَ مَادامَ التَّيارُ شَدِيدا.

There are certain verbs and particles which, when introduced at the beginning of a nominal sentence, bring about certain vowel changes in respect of their subject and predicate. Verbs of Incomplete Predication i.e. كَـانَ and its categories الأفْعَالُ النَّاقِصَة are discussed in this lesson.

The Verbs of Incomplete Predication الأفْعَالُ النَّاقِصَة * express the idea of becoming or state of continuation. When it is said كان أحمد *Ahmad was,* the person who hears this expression might as well ask: "What was Ahmad?". But, when it is stated كانَ أحمَد تاجِراً *Ahmad was a merchant,* the predicate is complete. This nominal sentence is analysed thus:

كَانَ is the verb of incomplete predication — كان - الفعل الناقص

أحمد is the subject of Kana — أحمد - إسـم كـانَ

تاجِراً is the predicate of Kana — تاجرا - خبر كان

According to the rules governing the subject and predicate in a nominal sentence, the vowels of the last letter of the two should be the same (see lesson No.9). But when كان and the verbs which fall under this category are added at the beginning of a nominal sentence:

1. The subject of كَانَ will be in the nominative case: مَرْفُوع ـُ
2. The predicate of كَانَ will be in the accusative case: مَنْصُوب ـَ

The list of الأفْعَالُ النَّاقِصَـة or كَانَ and its categories are given below:

---

* Literal meaning : *the incomplete verbs*

1. *to be*	كَانَ	2. *to become*	صَارَ
3. *to become (at dawn)*	أصبح	4. *not to be*	لَيْسَ
5. *as long as*	مَا دامَ	6. *to continue to*	مَا بَرِحَ
7. *to become in the forenoon*	أضْحَى	8. *to become in the evening*	أمْسَى
9. *to become during night*	بَاتَ	10. *to remain*	ظـــلَّ
11. *to continue*	مَافَتِيَ	12. *to continue*	مَا انفَكَّ
13. *to continue*	مَازَال		

In the following chart, the nominal sentences are written without and with كَانَ and its other categories. Note the vowel changes that occur as a result of the addition of كَانَ or verbs belonging to its group.

The boy was sick.	كَانَ الولدُ مَرِيْضـــاً	كَانَ	الْوَلَدُ مَرِيْضُ
The weather became hot.	صَارَ الجَوُ حَارًّا	صَار	الجَوُّ حَارٌّ
Rain became abundant at dawn.	اسبحَ المطرُ غزيرا	أَصبَحَ	المَطَرُ غَزيرٌ
The traveler became tired (at noon).	أضْحَى المُسَافِرُ متْعِبا	أضحَى	المُسافرُ مُتْعِبٌ
The boy became happy (in the evening).	أمسى الولَدُ مَسْرُوراً	أمْسَى	الوَلَدُ مَسْرُور
The patient slept during the night	بات المريض نائما	بات	المريض نائم
The soldier remained brave.	ظَلَّ الجُندِيُّ شُجاعاً	ظَلَّ	الجُندِيُّ شجاعٌ
The building is not strong.	لَيسَ البناءُ قويًّا	لَيسَ	البِنَاء قويٌّ

Hatim continues to be rich.	مازَال مَازالَ حاتِمْ غَنياً	حاتِم غَنِيٌّ
The worker continues to be hardworking.	مافتِئ مَافتِئ العَاملُ مُجتهداً	العامِلُ مُجتِهدٌ
The merchant continues to be trustworthy.	مانفكَّ مانفكَّ التَّاجِرُ صَادِقاً	التاجِرُ صَادِقٌ

First Category: كَـانَ , صَارَ , أصْبَحَ , أضْحَى , أمْسَى , بَاتَ and ظَـلَّ are converted to المَـاضِي *past tense* , المُضَـارع present tense, الأمْرُ *imperative,* الإسمُ الفاعِل *the active participle* and المصْدَر *verbal noun.*

Second category: مَـلزَال , مَا فَتِئَ , مَا بَرِحَ and مَـا انفكَّ are converted to المَاضِي , المُضَارع , and الإسمُ الفاعِل

Third category: لَيْـسَ and مَادامَ are not converted to المُضَارع , الأمْرُ and الإسمُ الفاعِل

The rules governing the use of كَانَ and verbs belonging to its category have been explained. These verbs are used to convey the idea of duration and continuity. It has to be noted that some verbs of this category,

a) are not in frequent use
b) nor are they used in their exact literal sense.

أصْبَـحَ literally means *"to become in the morning"* but it could also mean *"to become", "grow", "reach a state," "come to a point where.."* . In this sentence اصبحَ الفَلاَّحُ سعِيداً بِثمَرِ جُهُودِهِ *"The peasant has become happy with the fruit of his labor",* أصبحَ means *"has become",* duration is not indicated.

Conjugation of كَانَ *"To Be"*

Future & Present tense	المُضارع		Past tense		الـمَـاضـي	
Plural	Dual	Sing.	Plural	Dual	Sing.	
يكُونُون	يَكُونَانِ	يَكُونُ	كَانُوا	كَانَا	كَانَ	3rd Per.Mas.
يَكُـنَّ	تَكُونَانِ	تَكُونُ	كُـنَّ	كَانَتَا	كَانَتْ	3rd Per. Fem.
تَكُنُونَ	تَكُونَانِ	تَكُونُ	كُنْتُمْ	كُنْتُمَا	كُنْتَ	2nd Per. Mas.
تَكُـنَّ	تَكُونَانِ	تَكُنِيْنَ	كُنْتُـنَّ	كُنْتُمَا	كُنْتِ	2nd Per. Fem.
نكُون	نكُون	أكون	كنَّا	كنّا	كنتُ	1st Per Mas/ Fem.

يكُوْنُ	*he will be*	كَانَ	*he was*
لاَ تَكُنْ	*you do not be*	كُنْ	*you be*

كان is also used to form (1) "past continuous" e.g. كَان يذّهبُ *he was going/ he used to go* and (2) "distant past" كَان ذهبَ *he had gone.*

VOCABULARY

g̃ariqa	غرق	mutarjim	مترجم
to sink, plunge		*translator*	
istag̃raqa	إستغرق ؛ يستغرق	jamad, jãmid	جمد : جامد
to engage, absorb		*to freeze, solid*	
harwala	هرول ؛ يهرول	sayyãl	سيـــال
to hasten, walk fast		*liquid*	
anqada	أنقذ ؛ ينقذ	munãqasha	مناقشة
to rescue, save		*discussion, debate*	
ṣaḥĩḥ	صحيح	riyãḍi	رياضي
correct, healthy, right		*sportsman, mathematician*	

ḡalaṭ غلط
incorrect, mistake, wrong

aḵraja أخرج
to send out, bring out

ḵirrīj خريج
graduate (of a college)

musajjil مسجل
registrar, tape recorder

ḥallāq حلاق
barber

ḵayyāṭ خياط
tailor

muṣawwir مصور
photographer

tayyār تيار : مجرى
current, tide, course

tayyār mutanāwib تيار متناوب
alternating current

tayyār mubāshir تيار مباشر
direct current

wa'ada وعد
to promise

mau'id موعد
appointed time, pledge

riyāḍa رياضة : تمرين
exercise, practice

kanīsa كنيسة
synagogue, temple, church

ḡāya غاية : غرض
goal, aim, intent

mauqid موقد
stove

furn فرن
oven

mashwara مشورة : مشاورة
consultation, advice

mastashār مستشار : ناصح
adviser, chancellor

ṭāba yaumakum طاب يومكم
good day

ḥaẓẓan sayidan حظا سعيدا
good luck

qurrat al ain قرة العين
darling, delight of the eye

ittahama إتهم
to accuse

muttaham متهم
accused person, defendant

ḍidd ضد
contrary, opponent

miṣbāh مصباح
lamp

lā mani' لا مانع
no objection

mana'a منع ؛ يمنع
to prevent, hinder

mamnū' ممنوع
prohibited, banned

wahm وهم
suspicion, doubt

nizā نزاع
dispute, struggle

'āṣifa عاصفة
storm, tempest

faḍl فضل : إحسان
favour, kindness

jāmid جامد
hard, solid, frozen

furṣa d̲ahabiya فرصة ذهبية
golden opportunity

shāṭir شاطر
cunning, smart

tuhma تهمة
accusation, charge

bari برئ
guiltless, free from

mu'tamar مؤتمر
conference, convention

mustamir مستمر
continuous, lasting

qanāh قناة : ترعة
canal, tube

faiḍān فيضان
flood

hadaf هدف
target, objective, goal

muwāṣala مواصلة
communication

irtifā' إرتفاع
increase, height

sawāsiya سواسية
equal, alike

furshat asnaan فرشة أسنان
toothbrush

mumkin ممكن
possible

farra	فر ؛ يفر	mustaḥīl	مستحيل : غير ممكن
to escape, flee		*impossible*	
fāriḡ	فارغ	d̠ak̠ara	ذخر : إذخر
empty, not occupied		*to store, to keep*	
infijār	إنفجار	d̠ak̠īra	ذخيرة
explosion, outbreak		*treasure, supplies*	
marhūn	مرهون	mas'ūliya	مسئولية
mortgaged		*responsibility*	
muzdaḥim	مزدحم	mas'ūl	مسئول
crowded		*responsible, accountable*	

Note the use of كان and allied verbs in the following sentences.

TRANSLATION	*MODEL SENTENCES*
1. The garden was open.	١-كَانَتْ الحَدِيقة مَفْتُوحَة.
2. The wind became cold.	٢-صَار الهَوَاءُ بارداً.
3. Zaki is not sick.	٣-ليسَ ذَكِيٌّ مَرِيضاً.
4. Lakshmi is not lazy.	٤-ليسَتْ لكْشمِي كَسلانَة.
5. Water became frozen (at dawn).	٥-أصْبَحَ المَاءُ جَامِدًا.
6. The day became hot (in the forenoon).	٦-أضْحَى اليَوْمُ حَارًّا.
7. The flower became withered (in the evening).	٧-أمْسَى الزَّهرُ ذَابلاً.
8. The dog remained watchful.	٨- ظلَّ الكَلبُ حَارساً.

9. The watchman was standing (during night).	٩-باتَ الحَارسُ قائِماً.
10. Hamid is still in Iraq.	١٠- لا يزَالُ حامِد في العِـــرَاق.
11. He has enjoined upon me prayer and almsgiving, so long as I remain alive.	١١- أوصَـــانِي بـــالصَّلوةِ والزَّكـــوة مادُمتُ حَيًّا.
12. The wind continues to be strong.	١٢- ما فتِئتْ الرِّيحُ شدِيدَةً.
13. The market continues to be crowded.	١٣- ما انفكَّ السُّوق مُزدَحماً.
14. The airplane was about to explode.	١٤- كَادتْ الطَّيارةُ تنْفجِرُ.
15. Success is not easy.	١٥- لا نَجَاحَ سَهْلاً.
16. The army started moving.	١٦- شَرَعَ الْجَيشُ يَتَحرَّك.
17. Friendship without sincerity is not permanent.	١٧- لاَ صَداقة دَائِمَةً بِغير إخْلاَصٍ.
18. The student (f) started preparing for the examination.	١٨- أخَذَت التِّلْمِيْذَةُ تَسْتَعِدُّ لِلإمْتِحَانِ.
19. India became a great nation after Independence.	١٩- أصْبحَتْ الهِنْدُ دَولَةً كُبرَى بَعـــدَ الإسْتِقْلاَل
20. The playground is not crowded with people.	٢٠- لَيْسَ مَيْدَانُ اللَّعِبِ مُزْدَحماً مِـــن النَّـــاس.
21. The people remain marching on the way to progress.	٢١- سَيظَلُّ الشَّعبُ سَائِرا فِي طَرِيــق الرُّقي والتَّقدُّم.
22. The patient is still in the hospital.	٢٢- مَا زَال المَرِيضُ في المُسْتَشْفَى.

23. The train was slow near the station.	٢٣- كَان القِطَارُ بَطِيئا قُربَ المَحَطَّة.
24. The worker became tired in the evening.	٢٤- أمْسَى العَامِلُ مُتعبًا.
25. The lamp was burning at night.	٢٥- بَاتَ المِصْبَاحُ مُتَّقداً.
26. You will not succeed as long as you are lazy.	٢٦- لَنْ تنْجَحَ مَا دُمْتَ كَسلاَناً.
27. When He decreed a matter He says to it "Be" and it is.	٢٧- وإذا قضى أمرا فإنَّما يقول لــه كن فيكون.
28. We don't have much time.	٢٨- وليس أمامنا وقت طويل.
29. People had imagined that aviation was an impossible skill.	٢٩- كان النــاس يظنّــون أن فــن الطيران مستحيل.
30. Scientists are still engaged in exploring the secrets of the universe.	٣٠- ما زال العلماء يبحثــون عــن أسرار الكون.

LESSON TWENTY-ONE

إن **and its Categories** إن وأخواتهـا

THE BANKS | المصارف (البنوك)

1. Banks are very essential in every country.

١ - إنَّ المصارفَ ضرورية في كل بلد.

2. They (banks) keep (in safe custody) money and benefit the merchants and others by undertaking conversion of money into different currencies.

٢ - لأنها تحفظ الأموال وتفيد التجـار وغيرهم وتقوم بتحويل النقود إلـى عملات مختلفـة.

3. If only the highly rich recognized its utility.

٣ - وليت كبـارَ الأغنيـاء يعـترفون برسالتها.

4. But some of them are afraid of government interference in their affairs (conduct).

٤ - لكن بعضَهم خـائف مـن تدخـل الحكومة في معاملاتهم.

5. If only the government supervised their transactions completely in the interest of the people.

٥ -ولعل الدولةَ مشرفة عليها إشـرافا كاملا لمصلحة الشعب.

6. (And) the employees of the banks are polite.

٦ -وموظفوا المصارف قوم مهذبون.

7. It is necessary on the part of every individual to deposit (keep) a part of his income in the bank so that we can build our country and the deposits will be helpful to us (at the time of) need.

٧ -فعلى كل فرد أن يدخرَ جـزءا مـن دخله في البنك حتى نبنـي بلدنـا ويكون عونـا لنا عند الحاجـة.

When إن and its categories are added to a nominal sentence, the meaning of the sentence changes and also the vowels of their subject and predicate. الـهرم قديـم means *the pyramid is old,* but with the addition of إنَّ , as in أنَّ الهَرَمَ قدِيمٌ the sentence would mean *certainly the pyramid is old.* This sentence is analyzed as follows:

إنَّ	*certainly*	الحرف المشبَّه بالفِعل	The particles which resembles the verb
الهَرَمَ	*pyramid*	اسمُ إنَّ	the subject of إنَّ
قدِيمٌ	*old*	خبرُ إنَّ	the predicate of إنَّ

The particles bring about a vowel change in their subject and predicate.

1. The subject of إنَّ will be in the accusative case ـَ مَنْصُوب
2. The predicate of إنَّ will be in the nominative case ـُ مَرْفُوع

The particles which are called إنَّ and its sisters are as follows, and all these have been used in the illustrative text above (page 136)

perhaps	(٥) لعَلَّ	*as if*	(٣) كَأنَّ	*certainly*	(١) إنَّ
if only	(٦) لَيْتَ	*but*	(٤) لكِنَّ	*that*	(٢) أنَّ

VOCABULARY

quwat as-shirā	قوة الشراء	ṭalab	طلب
purchasing power		*demand, claim*	
mablag̃	مبلغ	'inda ṭalab	عند الطلب
a sum, amount		*on demand*	
al majmū'	المجموع	maṭlūb	مطلوب
the total		*wanted, due*	
irtifā' al as'ār	إرتفاع الأسعار	dain	ديـن – ديون
price rise		*debt, liability*	

takfīḍ al as'ār تخفيض الأسعار
price reduction

ṣāfi al humūla صافي الحمولة
net tonnage

mīzāniya ميزانية
balance sheet, budget

sharīk شريك – شركاء
partner

ishtirāk إشتراك
partnership, subscription

sharika شركة
company, establishment

taqsīt تقسيط
payment in installments

sahm سهم
share

musāhim مساهم
shareholder

barṣa برصة
stock exchange

gumruk جمرك – جمارك
custom house

rusūm al gumruk رسوم الجمرك
customs duty, tariff

shirā شراء
purchase

bai' بيع
sale

bai' bil jumla بيع بالجملة
wholesale

bai' bil mufrad بيع بالمفرد
retail

al bai' naqdan البيع نقدا
cash sale

al bai' diana البيع دينا
credit sale

taṣfiya تصفية
liquidation

namūḏaj نموذج
pattern, model, sample

rusūm ash shahn رسوم الشحن
the freight

makus مكس – مكوس
excise duty, tax

dafātir دفاتر : سجلات
journals, ledgers

maktab مكتب
office, bureau

dafa` دفعة

payment, thrust

ḥisāb حساب

accounting, calculation

ḥisāb jāri حساب جار

current account

ḥisāb al taufir حساب التوفير

savings account

taswiya تسوية

settlement

taflīs تفليس

bankruptcy

tarīḍ al k̲asāra تعريض الخسارة

indemnity

ribh ربح

interest, benefit

fāida فائدة

profit, use

k̲asāra خسارة

loss, damage

dak̲l دخل

income, receipts

ras māl رأس مال

capital amount

kātib كاتب

clerk, typist

ṣarrāf صراف

cashier, money changer

musā'id مساعد

assistant

wakīl وكيل

agent, sponsor

wakāla وكالة : تفويض

agent, sponsor

biḍā'a بضاعة : متاع

goods, commodities

fātura فاتورة

invoice, bill

waṣl وصل : إيصال

voucher, receipt

'umla ṣa'ba عملة صعبة

hard currency

'umla sahla عملة سهلة

soft currency

tauqī' توقيع

signature

naqd نقد - نقود

ready money, cash

istismār إستثمار
investment, utilization
nafaqa نفقة – نفقات
expenditure, outlay
bulsat ash shahn بولسة الشحن
bill of lading
'alāma علامة : مارك
mark, emblem
riyāl ريال
Saudi Arabian currency
dīnār دينار
Iraqi and Kuwaiti currency
dirham درهم
Gulf States currency
fils فلس – فلوس
small coins
dolār دولار
dollar
mustauda' مستودع
warehouse, storehouse
musāwama مساومة
bargaining
kambiyāla كمبيالة
bill of exchange, draft

fakka فكـــة
small coins
istiqdām إستقدام
recruitment
al ayde al'āmila الأيدي العاملة
manpower, workers
'arḍ عرض
offer, display, supply
ma'riḍ معرض
showroom, exhibition
k̲azāna خزانة
treasury, locker
mak̲zan مخزن : دكان : محل
store, shop
taṣdīr تصدير : صادرات
export, sending
taurīd توريد : واردات
import, supply
tamwīl تمويل
financing
ālat al kitāba آلة الكتابة
typewriter
mu'āmala معاملة
transaction, conduct

ḥawala حوالة
promissory note

mazād مزاد
auction

munaqaṣa مناقصة
tender

muwāfaqa موافقة
approval, sanction

rahn رهن
mortgage

'umūlah عمولة
commission, brokerage

ilḡa إلغاء : إنهاء
cancellation, termination

simsār سمسار
broker, middleman

ḍarība ضريبة - ضرائب
tax, duty

ḍarībat ad-dak̲l ضريبة الدخل
income tax

ḍarībat kasb ضريبة كسب العمل
wage tax

taṣdīq تصديق
attestation, ratification

tadak̲k̲ul تدخل
interference, intervention

muwaẓẓaf موظف
employee

sharṭ شرط - شروط
condition

'aqd عقد : معاهدة
contract, agreement

qarḍ قرض
loan

taḥwīl تحويل
conversion, transfer

taswīq تسويق
marketing, sale

waraqat 'itimād ورقة إعتماد
credit card

wat̲iqa, ṣakk وثيقة : صك
document, record

ḍarura ضرورة : حاجة
need, want

'uqubat iqtiṣādia عقوبات إقتصادية
economic sanctions

ik̲tiyār إختيار
selection, choice

Make a note the use of إن and allied particles in the following sentences.

TRANSLATION	*MODEL SENTENCES*
1. Certainly God is with the steadfast.	١ – إنَّ اللهَ مَعَ الصَّابِرين.
2. As if the news was correct!	٢ – كَأنَّ الخَبَرَ صَحِيح.
3. The plane crashed but the loss is little.	٣ – سقطت الطَّائِرَة لكِنَّ الخَسَارة قليلة.
4. If only the accused was free!	٤ – لَيتَ المتَّهم بَرِئ.
5. Perhaps the conference is continuing.	٥ – لَعَلَّ المُؤتَمَرَ مُستَمِر.
6. I know that fish are abundant in this pond.	٦ – أنا أعرف أنَّ السمكَ كَثِير في هذِه التُّرعة.
7. During the moon-lit night the water was shining as if it was silver.	٧ – كَأنَّ المَاءَ فِضَّة لامِعَة في ليلة مُقمرة.
8. Certainly Mumbai is the biggest port in India.	٨ – إنَّ مُمباي أكبر مِينَاء فِي الهندِ.
9. If only world peace was permanent!	٩ – ليتَ السَّلامَ العَالَمِي دَائِم.
10. Perhaps the train is reaching the station according to schedule.	١٠ – لَعَلَّ القِطارَ يَصِلُ المَحَطَّة فِي مَوعِدِه.
11. The tree is big but it is not bearing fruit.	١١ – الشَّجَرَة كَبِيرَة لكِنَّها غير مُثمِرَة.
12. We have no knowledge except that which You (God) had taught us.	١٢ – لا عِلْمَ لَنَا إلاَّ مَا عَلَّمْتَنَا.

13. Certainly the Taj Mahal is beautiful.	١٣- إنَّ تاج مَحَل جَميل.
14. It pleases me to participate in this party.	١٤- يَسُرُّنِي أن أشْتركَ في هَذِه الحَفلة.
15. The moon looked as if it was a lamp in the desert!	١٥- كَأنَّ القمَرَ مِصبَاح في الصَّحراء.
16. If only the medicine was useful!	١٦- ليتَ الدَّواء مُفيد.
17. Perhaps the culprit is free!	١٧- لعَلَّ المُجْرِمَ طَلِيق.
18. It pains me that the war is continuing.	١٨- يولِمُنِي أنَّ الحَربَ مُسْتَمِرَّة.
19. Certainly spring is not far away.	١٩- إنَّ الرَّبيعَ غيرَ بَعِيدٍ.
20. Perhaps the goal is near!	٢٠- لَعَلَّ الهَدَفَ قريب.
21. None who consults about his affairs is repentant.	٢١- لا مُسْتَشيرَ في أمُوره نادِماً.
22. No jealous person is comfortable.	٢٢- لا حَاسِدَ مُسْتَريحا.

LESSON TWENTY-TWO

The Numerals, Days and Months
أسماء العدد والأيام والشهور

CARDINALS

ten	عشرة	eleven	أحد عشر	one	واحد
twenty	عشرون	twelve	اثنا عشر	two	اثنان
thirty	ثلاثون	thirteen	ثلاثة عشر	three	ثلاثة
forty	أربعون	fourteen	أربعة عشر	four	أربعة
fifty	خمسون	fifteen	خمسة عشر	five	خمسة
sixty	ستون	sixteen	سِتَّة عشر	six	سِتَّة
seventy	سَبعُون	seventeen	سَبعَة عشر	seven	سَبعَة
eighty	ثمانُون	eighteen	ثمَانِية عشر	eight	ثمانِية
ninety	تِسعُون	nineteen	تِسْعَة عشر	nine	تِسعَة
hundred	مائة	twenty	عِشرُون	ten	عشرة

400	أربَع مائة	300	ثلاث مئة	200	مائتان
700	سبع مئة	600	ست مئة	500	خمس مئة
1,000	ألف	900	تسع مئة	800	ثماني مئة

ORDINALS

	Fem. مؤنث	Mas. مذكر
first	الأولـــى	الأول
second	الثانيـــة	الثانـــي
third	الثالثـــة	الثـــالـــث
fourth	الرابعـــة	الـــرابع
fifth	الخامسة	الخـــامس
sixth	السادسة	الســـادس
seventh	السابعـــة	الســـابع
eighth	الثامنة	الثـــامن
ninth	التاسعـــة	التـــاسع
tenth	العـــاشرة	العـــاشر

ربع	نصف	ثلث	خمس	سدس	واحد في المائة	مائة في المائـــة
١/٤	١/٢	١/٣	١/٥	١/٦	%١	%١٠٠

The numerals used in many parts of the world are known as "Arabic numerals" though the Arabs write these in a different way.

The Arabic numerals are:

١	٢	٣	٤	٥	٦	٧	٨	٩	٠
1	**2**	**3**	**4**	**5**	**6**	**7**	**8**	**9**	**0**

In handwritten texts the number two is written as "٢", صفر zero is indicated by a dot " ٠ ". Arabic is both written and read from right to left, but when writing numbers in Arabic, the English method is followed.e.g.

١١	٢٥	١٠١	١٩٧٠	٢٠٠٠
11	**25**	**101**	**1970**	**2000**

Note on the Syntax of the Numerals:

(1-2) The numerals 1 and 2 agree in gender with the noun to which they refer. e.g. ولد واحد *one boy* بنت واحدة *one girl.*

(3-10) These numerals disagree in gender with the singular of the noun counted, and put that noun in the genitive plural. e.g.

ثلاثة أولاد *three* (fem.) *boys* (mas.)

ثلاث بَنَاتٍ *three* (mas.) *girls* (fem.)

(11-12) Both parts of these numerals agree in gender with the noun, and the noun is put in the accusative singular. e.g.

أحد عشر رجلا *eleven men* إحدى عشرة إمرأة *eleven women*

(13-19) These are followed by the noun in the accusative singular. The unit disagrees in gender with its noun and with the word for "ten". e.g.

ثلاثة عشر رجلا *thirteen men* ثلاث عشرة إمرأة *thirteen women*

The numerals which indicate numbers made up of thousands, hundreds, tens and units may be read in two ways: number 1976 could be read as:

(1) ستة وسبعون وتسعمائة وألف

(2) ألف وتسعمائة وستة وسبعون

WEEKDAYS أيـــام الأسبـــوع

Wednesday	٤- يوم الأربعـــاء	Sunday	١- يوم الأحـــد
Thursday	٥- يوم الخميس	Monday	٢- يوم الإثنين
Friday	٦- يوم الجمعة	Tuesday	٣- يوم الثلاثاء
Saturday	٧- يوم السبت		

MONTHS OF THE HIJRI YEAR أشهر السنة الهجرية

١	- محرم	٧	- رجب
٢	- صفر	٨	- شعبان
٣	- ربيع الأول	٩	- رمضان
٤	- ربيع الاخر	١٠	- شوال
٥	- جمادى الأولى	١١	- ذو القعدة
٦	- جمادى الآخرة	١٢	- ذو الحجة

MONTHS OF THE CHRISTIAN YEAR أشهر السنة الميلادية

	Syrian name	Egyptian name
January	كانون الثاني*	١- يناير*
February	شباط	٢- فبراير
March	آذار	٣- مارس
April	نيسان	٤- ابريل
May	آيار	٥- مايو
June	حزيران	٦- يونيه
July	تموز	٧- يوليه
August	آب	٨- أغسطس
September	أيلول	٩- سبتمبر
October	تشرين الأول	١٠- أكتوبر
November	تشرين الثاني	١١- نوفمبر
December	كانون الأول	١٢- ديسمبر

* It is usual to use both the names together for the purpose of clarity.

TIME الـوقت

one o`clock	الســاعة الــواحــدة
quarter past one	الــواحدة والــربــع
half past one	الــواحدة والنصف
quarter to two	الثــانية إلا الــربع
half past seven	السابعــة والنصف
quarter to nine	التــاسِعة إلا الربــع
five minutes past nine	التَّاسعة وخمس دقــائــق
twenty minutes past eleven	الحادية عشرة وعشرون دقائق

LESSON TWENTY-THREE

Types of Nouns Derived from Verbs

تقسيم الاسم إلي مصدر وجامد ومشتق

Nouns and its varieties have been dealt with in the earlier lessons of this book. The discussion in this lesson concerns nouns derived from the verbs, which come very near to Gerunds and Participles in English.

Arab grammarians have classified Nouns into three groups.

1. إسـم المصـدر "The Verbal Noun" properly expresses the verbal idea in the form of a noun. It is the root (of a word) from which proceed the verb, and its derivatives are formed from the root (radical letters) of a word,

حِرْفَـة	إمْتِنَاع	اضْطِرَابٌ	سَيْرٌ	صَوْتٌ
profession	*forbidding*	*striking*	*walking*	*sound*
لَون	مَرْضٌ	سُهُولة	فَصَاحَةٌ	فَرْحُ
color	*malady*	*easiness*	*eloquence*	*happiness*
قُعُودٌ	فَتْحٌ	زِرَاعة	مَوْعِد	مَوقع
sitting	*opening*	*agriculture*	*engagement*	*situation*

2. إسـم الجـامد It is a noun which is "stationary" or " incapable of growth". In other words it is a noun which is not derived from any word; neither is any word derived from it. e.g.

جَعْفَر	رَجُلٌ	فَرْسٌ
Jafar	*man*	*horse*

3. اسم المشـتق It is a noun which is derived from a verbal root. The following are formed from the verb فَتَحَ *to open.*

مِفتَـاحٌ	مَفْتُوحٌ	فَاتِحٌ
key	*opened*	*opener*

There are six forms of nouns which are derived from the verbal root.

1. Active participle إسم الفاعـــل
2. Passive participle إسم المفعول
3. Adjectives which are الصفة المشبه باسم الفاعل
   assimilated to the active participle.
4. The Noun of pre-eminence إسم التفضيل
5. The Noun denoting instruments إسم الآلـــة
6. The Noun of time and place إسم الزمان والمكان

The nouns which the Arab grammarians call إسم الفاعل *Active participle* and إسم المفعول *Passive participle,* are verbal adjectives, i.e. adjectives derived from verbs and nearly correspond in meaning to what are known as participles in the English language. A nominal sentence which consists of a subject and a predicate generally has either of these as predicate.

1. THE ACTIVE PARTICIPLE إســم الفــاعل

It denotes the person who does the act or is responsible for it. It is formed from the verb in the past tense, 3rd person, by adding *Alif* after the first radical and adding *kasrah* ـِ to the second radical, i.e. in the form of فـــاعِل e.g.

قَاتِلٌ	نَافِــع	فَــاعِــلٌ	كَاتِبٌ	عَــالِمٌ	شَــاكِرٌ
killer	*useful*	*doer*	*writer*	*knower*	*thankful*

This rule is only applicable for triliteral verbs (verbs with three radical letters). There are different rules for quadriliteral verbs.

2. THE PASSIVE PARTICIPLE إسم المفعول

It denotes the person or a thing towards which the action is extended. It is formed by prefixing م with *Fatha* ـَ to the verb in the past tense, 3rd person and adding و after the second radical i.e. in the form of مفعول . e.g.

مفعول	مكتوب	معلوم	مجهول
a thing done	*written*	*known*	*unknown*

This rule is for triliteral verbs. For quadriliteral verbs there are different rules.

3. ADJECTIVES WHICH ARE ASSIMILATED TO THE ACTIVE PARTICIPLE الصفة المشبهة بإسم الفاعل

This is formed from the intransitive verbs. It expresses a quality inherent and permanent in a person or thing without any limitation. It is used to convey a certain degree of intensity. In this respect it is slightly different from إسم الفاعل *the active participle.* e.g.

hard	(صلب) صلب	*handsome*	(حسن) حسن	*red*	(حمر) أحمر
noble	(شرف) شرف	*brave*	(شجع) شجاع	*black*	(سود) أسود

4. NOUNS OF PRE-EMINENCE AND DEGREES OF COMPARISON إسم التفضيل

This is used when it is intended to express that one person or thing surpasses others in possessing a certain quality. This is usually formed on the pattern of فعل . e.g.

1. Knowledge is more useful than wealth. ١ - العلم أنفع من المال.
2. Ahmad is older than Najeeb. ٢ - أحمد أكبر من نجيب.
3. Khalid is more clever than Sayeed. ٣ - خالد أذكى من سعيد.

4. The West is more advanced than the East. ٤- الغرب أكثر تقدُّما من الشرق.

The Superlative degree is used in the following sentences.

5. The book is the best companion. ٥- الكِتاب أفضل جليس.

6. Truly, the most worthy of honor in the sight of God is he who fears Him most. ٦- إنَّ أكرمكم عِندَ اللهِ أتْقاكُمْ.

5 THE NOUN DENOTING THE INSTRUMENT OF THE ACT

اسم الآلــة

A noun which denotes the instrument that one uses in performing the act (expressed by a verb) is called in Arabic, إسم الآلة. This is formed by prefixing م with *Kasra* ـِ, to the verb in the past tense, 3rd person. It has three different forms:

a stick	مِضْرَبٌ	*a plough*	مِزْرَعٌ	*a needle*	١- مِفْعَلٌ < مِخيط
a net	مِصْيَدَةٌ	*a broom*	مِكْنَسَةٌ	*a fan*	٢- مِفْعلَةٌ < مِروَحَةٌ
a lamp	مِصباَح	*a saw*	مِنْشارٌ	*a key*	٣- مِفْعَالٌ < مِفْتــاحُ

6 NOUN OF PLACE OR TIME اسم الظرف

A noun which indicates the time or place of occurrence of an act is called in Arabic اسم الظرف. It is also called اسم الظرف والمكان . This is formed by prefixing م with *Fatha* ـَ to the verb in the past tense, 3rd person. e .g.

مَسْجِــدٌ	مَنْــزِلٌ	مَغْــرِبٌ	مَشْــرِقٌ
where prayer is offered *(mosque)*	stopping place *(house)*	where the sun sets *(west)*	where the sun rises *(east)*

LESSON TWENTY-FOUR

Derived Forms of the Verb

الفعل المجرد والمزيد

The great majority of the Arabic verbs are triliteral, i.e. they consist of three radical letters only. The quadriliteral verbs, which consist of four radical letters are less in number.

The triliteral verbs are of two kinds:

(1) Those which contain merely three radical letters which are known as الثلاثي المجرد . e.g. خرجَ *to go out.*

(2) Those which contain one, two or three additional letters besides the three radical letters. These are known as الثلاثي المزيد فيه. e.g. أخرَجَ *to send out.* These in fact are "the derived forms of the triliteral verbs". They differ from the original, in meaning to some extent. In the Arabic dictionaries, the triliteral verb is listed first and the meanings of its derived forms follow one after another.

There are twelve forms of triliteral verbs.

A. Forms increased by one letter:

١- أفعلُ   خَرَجَ - أخْرَجَ   ٢- فعَّلَ   ضرَبَ - ضرَّبَ

٣- فَاعَلَ   قتَلَ - قاتل

B. Forms increased by two letters:

٤- تفعَّلَ   قبلَ - تقبَّلَ   ٥- تفاعَلَ   قتَلَ - تقاتَلَ

٦- افتَعلَ   جَنَبَ - اجتَنَبَ   ٧- انْفعَلَ   فطرَ - انْفطرَ

٨- افعَلَّ   حمرَ - احْمرَّ

C. Forms increased by three letters:

٩- افعالَّ   دهمَ - ادهامَّ   ١٠- استفْعلَ   نصرَ - استنْصرَ

١١- افعوعَلَ   خشُنَ - اخْشَوشنَ   ١٢- افعوَّلَ   جلدَ - اجلوَّدَ

Details about each of the above forms of derived verbs:

I. أفعـل. This is formed by prefixing *Hamza* أ as a result of which the first radical loses its vowel. It implies "causing an act"

To make one sit أجلس *to sit* جلسَ

*١ – أجلس ٢ – يُجلِس ٣ – أجلس ٤ – لا تجلس ٥ – إجلاسا

٦ – مجلس ٧ – مجلس

II. فعّـلَ. The second form is formed by doubling the second radical. It implies that an act is done with intensity.

To teach علّم *to know* علِم

١ – علّم ٢ – يُعلّم ٣ – علّم ٤ – لا تعلم ٥ – تعليما

٦ – معلّم ٧ – معلّم

III. فـاعلَ. This is formed by the introduction of *Alif* after the first radical. This expresses the effort to perform the act upon the object

To try to kill قاتل *to kill* قتل

١ – قاتل ٢ – يُقاتل ٣ – قاتل ٤ – لا تقاتل ٥ – مقاتلة

٦ – مقاتِل ٧ – مقاتَل

IV. تفعّـلَ. This is formed by prefixing ت and doubling the second radical. This adds reflexive force to the original verb.

To be broken into تكسّر *to break* كسر

١ – تكسّر ٢ – يتكسّر ٣ – تكسّر ٤ – لا تتكسّر ٥ – تكسّرا

٦ – متكسّر ٧ – متكسّر

---

*Under each form of the derived verbs, the following are shown: (1) Past tense (2) Imperfect (3) Imperative (4) Negative command (5) Verbal noun Gerund (6) Active participle noun (7) Passive participle noun

V. تفاعَل. This is formed by prefixing ت and by adding *Alif* before the second radical. The idea of reflexive action is conveyed through this form.

to fight one another تقاتَل *to kill* قتل

١ – تقاتل ٢ – يتقاتل ٣ – تقاتل ٤ – لا تتقاتل ٥ – تقاتلا

٦ – متقاتل ٧ – متقاتَل

VI. اِفْتَعَل. This is formed by prefixing ا *Hamzat al wasal* and adding ت after the first radical which loses its vowel.

to avoid اجتنب *to avert* جنب

١ – اجتنب ٢ – يجتنب ٣ – اجتنِبْ ٤ – لا تجتنِبْ ٥ – اجتِنابا

٦ – مجتنِب ٧ – مجتنَبٌ

VII. انفعَل. This is formed by prefixing ا and ن. It has a reflexive signification. It is generally used as passive.

to be split انفَطَر *to split* فطر

١ – انفطر ٢ – ينفطر ٣ – انفطِر ٤ – لا تنفطر ٥ – انفِطارا

٦ – منفطِر

VIII. افعلَّ. This is formed by prefixing ا *Hamzat al wasal* and doubling the third radical. It is used to express colors and defects.

to become red إحمَرَّ *to make red* حمر

١ – إحمَرَّ ٢ – يحْمَرُّ ٣ – إحمَرِرْ ٤ – لا تحمَرِرْ ٥ – إحمِرِرَارا

٦ – محْمرٌّ

IX. إفعالّ. This is formed by prefixing *Hamza* إ and adding *Alif* after the second radical and doubling the third. This too is used to express colors.

to be black إدهامٌّ *to blacken* دهم

١ – إدهامَّ ٢ – يدهامُّ ٣ – إدهامِمْ ٤ – لا تدهامِمْ ٥ – إدهيماما

٦ – مدهامٌّ

X. استفعل. This form has a reflexive signification, it modifies the meaning of the root form by adding to it the idea of "desiring" and "asking".

to ask for support إستنصر *to support* نصر

١ – إستنصر ٢ – يستنصر ٣ – إستنصر ٤ – لا تستنصر ٥ – إستنصارا

٦ – مستنصر ٧ – مستنصر

Forms No. XI and XII are rarely used.

THE QUADRILITERAL VERBS

The verbs which contain four radical letters are called رباعي. These are of two kinds:

I. Those which consist of merely four radicals and are known as مجرد رباعي.

II. Those which consist of one or two letters in addition to the four radicals are called مزيد الرباعي.

Examples of the first category:

دحْرَجَ	وَسْوَسَ	زَلْزَلَ	جَمْهَرَ	هَرْوَلَ
to roll	*to whisper*	*to shake*	*to collect*	*to rush*

١ – دحرَجَ ٢ – يدحرِجُ ٣ – دحْرِجْ ٤ – لا تدحْرِجْ ٥ – دحْـرجةً

٦ – مدحْرِجٌ ٧ – مدحْرَجٌ

The derived forms of the quadriliteral verbs are:

١– تفَعْلَلَ (تدحرج) ٢– إفْعَنْلَلَ (إحرنجم) ٣– إفعلل (إقشَعرَّ)

LESSON TWENTY-FIVE

The Particles الحروف

There are four kinds of particles, حروف:

(1) Prepositions (2) Adverbs (3) Conjunctions and (4) Interjections.

CONJUNCTIONS – حروف العطف

The conjunctions are either (a) Separable or (b) Inseparable.

(a) The examples of separable conjunctions are:

(1) لكن *but* الكتاب صغير لكن نفعه عظيم

(2) ثمَّ *then, thereupon* زرعنا القطن ثم جنيناه

(b) Among the inseparable conjunctions و *and, also* ف *and so, and then* are widely used. و joins two independent words or sentences, whereas ف , which usually joins sentences only, indicates a development in the narrative. e.g.

(1) اكلت التفاح والعنب (2) دخل المدرس فوقف التلاميذ

INTERJECTIONS – حروف النداء

The particles which are widely used as interjections are يا and يا أيُّها meaning "Oh" e.g. يا ولد *Oh boy!* يا أيُّها المؤمنون *Oh, believers!*

PARTICLES

Prepositions and words which are used as such:

to	ل	within	داخل	to, until	إلى
at, which	لدى	without	دون	in front of, before	أمام
from	من	on, above	على	with, by	ب
without	من غير	of, from, about	عن	after	بعد
since	منذ	with	عند	between, among	بين
with	مع	instead of	عوض	by (in swearing)	ت
by (in swearing)	و	except	غير	under	تحت

behind	وراء	in	في	next, near	جنب
middle of	وسط	above	فوق	until, even to	حتى
besides	وسوى	before	قبل	round, around	حول
after, behind	خلف	opposite	قدام	outside	خارج

ADVERBS

(a) The adverbs which are used as interrogatives are mentioned in lesson No.13.

(b) *Adverbs of place:*

here	هاهنا	here	هنا	outside	برا
on top	فوق	there	هناك	inside	جوا
down, below	تحت	there	هنالك	wherever	أينما

(c) *Adverbs of time:*

now	الآن	early, tomorrow	بكرة	today	اليوم
ever, never	قط	late	متأخرا	yesterday	البارحة
immediately, directly	مباشرة	ever, never	أبدا	the day before yesterday	أول البارحة
tomorrow	غدا	always	دائما	yesterday	أمس
afterwards	بعد	immediately	حالا	earlier	سابقا

(c) *Adverbs of Quality*:

without	بدون	a little, a bit	شوية	very much	كثيرا
enough	كفاية	a small quantity	قليل	much, most	جدا

(e) *Adverbs of Affirmation*:

together with	معا	thus, so	كذا	yes	نعم
nearly	كفاية	together	جميعا	thus, so	هكذا

Second Part

SELECTIONS FROM

MODERN ARABIC LITERATURE

PROSE AND POETRY

الجزء الثاني

مختارات من الأدب العربي الحديث

شعـــر ونثـــر

١ - الإنسانية العامـــة

مصطفى لطفي المنفلوطي
١٨٧٦ - ١٩٢٤

١ - ليس لصاحب وطنٍ من الأوطان أو صاحب دين من الأديـــان أن يقول لغيره مـــمن يَسكنُ وطنا غيـــرَ وطنه، أو يَدينُ بدينٍ غيْر دينـــه : أنا غيـــرك، فيجب أن أكون عدوَّك؛ لأنَّ الإنسانية وحـــدةٌ لا تكثُّر [١] فيها ولا غيـــريَّة ولأن هذه الفروق التِي توجدُ بين الناس فِي آرائِهم ومذاهبهم، ومواطن إقامتهم وألـــوان أجســـادهم وأطوالِـــهم وأعراضهم - إنَّما هي اعتباراتٌ ومُصطلحاتٌ أو مُصادفاتٌ وإتفاقـــاتٌ، تعرِضُ لجوهر الإنسانية بعد تكوينه واستتْمام خلقه، وتتوارد عليه تـــواردَ الأعراض[٢] علي الأجسام.

ولد مصطفى لطفي المنفلوطي بمنفلوط (مصر) وحفظ القرآن في حداثته ، ثـــم درس بلأزهر لمدة عشر سنوات. قرأ الكتب المترجَمة على عهده ولا سيما القصص الرومانسية. ومن هذه القراءة المتصلة تكون ذوقه الأدبي. ومِما يثير إليه في مقالاتـــه شغفه بشعر الهموم والأحزان، وموقف البـــؤس والشـــقاء، وقصـــص المكلومـــين والمنكوبين. فترعرعت نفسه علي حب الرحْمة والشعور مع الآخريـــن.

(١) لا تكثر فيها : التكثر طلب الكثرة

(٢) الأعراض : جمع عرض وهو ضد الجوهر

٢ – وإذا جاز لكل إقليم أن يتنكرَ لغيْره من الأقاليم جاز لكل بلـــد أن يتنكر لغيـــره من البلاد، بـــل جاز لكلِّ بيت أن ينظرَ تلـــك النظـــرةَ الشزراءَ [١] إلي البيت الذي يجاوره، بل جاز لـــلأب أن يقـــول لولـــده، وللولد أن يقول لأبيـــه: إليك عنِّـــي [٢] لا تَمُد عينيك إلي شيء مِمـــا في يدي، ولا تَطْمع أن أوثرك على نفسي بشيء مِما اختصصتها به؛ لأنـــي غيـــرُك فيجب أن أكون عدوّك الـــمحارب لك، وهناك تنحـــلّ كـــل عُقدة، وتنفصم كل عُروة، ويـــحمل كل إنسان لأخيه بين أضلاعه مـــن لواعجَ [٣] البغض والمقت ما يُرنّقَ [٤] عيشه، ويطيل سُـــهده ، ويُقلـــق مضجعه، ويُحبب إليه صورة الْموت ، ويُبغض إليه وجه الحياة. وهنـــالك يُصبح الإنسان أشبه بشيء بذلك الإنسان الأول في وحشته وانفـــراده، يُقلب وجهه في آفاق السماء، وينبش بيديه طبقات الأرض، فلا يجـــد في الوحشة مؤنسا، ولا على الهموم مُعيناً.

٣ – الجامعة الإنسانية أقرب الجامعات إلـــى قلب الإنسان ، وأعلقـــها بفؤاده، وألصقُها بنفسه ، لأنه يبكي لمصاب من لا يعـــرف ، وإن كـــان المصابُ تاريخا من التواريخ أو أسطورة من الأساطيْر ، لأنه لا يرى غريقا

---

(١) الشزراء : المستهينة المحتقرة
(٢) إليك عني : ابتعـــد
(٣) لواعج البغض : ما يحرق ويؤلم
(٤) يرنق عيشه : كدره وعكر صفاءه

يتخبط في الْماء أو حريقا يتلظى [١] في النار حتى تُحدِّثه نفسه بالمخاطرة في سبيله فيقف وقفة الحزين المتلهف إن كان ضعيفا، ويندفع اندفاع الشجاع المستقتل إن كان قويا ، ويَسمع وهو بالشرق حديث النكبات بالغرب فيخفق قلُبه ، وتطير نفسُه ؛ لأنه يعلم أن أولئك المنكوبين، إخوانه في الإنسانية وإن لم يكن بينه وبينهم صلةٌ في أمر سواها، ولو لا أن ستارا من الجهل والعصبية يُسبله [٢] كل يوم غُلاة الوطنية والدين أو تُجَّارهُما علي قلوب الضعفاء السُّذج لما عاش منكوب في هذه الحياة بلا راحم، ولا ضعيفٌ بلا معين.

٤ – لا بأس بالفكرة الوطنية ، ولا بأس بالحمية الدينية، ولا بأس بالعصبية لهما ، والذود عنهما ، ولكن يجب أن يكون ذلك في سبيل الإنسانية، وتحت ظلالها ، أي أن تكون دوائرَ الجامعات كلها داخلة في دائرة الإنسانية العامة ، غير خارجة عنها.

والوطنية لا تزال عملا من الأعمال الشريفة المقدّمة حتى تخرج عن حدود الإنسانية ، فإذا هي خيالاتٌ باطلةٌ وأوهام كاذبةٌ ، والدِّين لا زال

(١) حريقا يتلظى : يلتهب (٢) يُسبله : أرخاه

غريزةً من غرائز الخير المؤثِّرة في صلاح النفوس وهُداها ، حتى يتجـرّد [١] علي الإنسانية وينابذها [٢] فإذا هو شُعبة من شُعب الجنون.

٥- فإن كان لا بد للإنسان من أن يحارب أخاه أو يقاتله فليُحاربه مُدافعا لا مهاجِما ، وليقاتله مؤدبا لا منتقما ، وليكنْ موقفُه أمامـه في جميـع ذلك موقف العادل المنصف ، والشقيق الرحيم ، فيدفنـه قتيـلا ، ويعالجه جريْحا ، ويكرمه أسيـرا ، ويخلُفه علي أهله وولده بأفضل مـا يخلُف الرجل الكريْم أخاه الشقيق علي ولده من بعده ، وليكُـن شـأنه معه شأن تلك الفئة المتحاربة التى وصفها الشاعر بقوله :

إذا احتَربتْ[٣] يوما ففاضتْ[٤] دماؤها تذكَّرت القُربى ففاضَتْ دموعُها

---

(١) يتجرد علي الإنسانية : يخرج عليها ويحاربها (٢) نابذها : خالفها وفارقها من عداوة

(٣) إحترب القوم : أوقدوا نار الحرب بينهم (٤) فاضت : تدفقت

٢ - الديــن الصناعي

للدكتــور أحـــمد أمين
١٨٧٨ - ١٩٥٤

هل تعرف الفرق بين الحرير الطبيعي والحرير الصناعي؟ وهل تعـرف الفرق بين الأسد وصورة الأسد؟ وهل تعرف الفرق بين الدنيا في الخـارج والدنيا علي الخريطة؟ [١] وهل تعرف الفرق بين عملك في اليقظـــة وعملك في المنام؟ وهل تعرف الفرق بين إنسان يسعى في الحيـــاة، وبين إنسان من جبس [٢] وضع في متجر لتعرض عليه الملابس؟ وهـل تعرف الفرق بين النائحة الثكلى [٣] والنائحة المستأجرة، وبين التكحل في العينين والكحل [٤] ؟ وهل تعرف الفرق بين السيف يـــمسكه الجندي المـــحارب وبين السيف الخشبي يمسكه الخطيب يوم الجمعة؟ وهل تعرف

ولد أحمد أمين عام ١٨٧٨م في مدينة القاهرة ودخل الأزهر ومدرســـة القضـــاء الشرعي فتخرج بها قاضيا وتعلم الإنكليزية واشتهر ببحوثه الأدبيـــة ومقالاتـــه العلمية. من أشهر مؤلفاته وأعظمها إنتشارا سلسلة كتب "فجر الإسلام" و "ضحى الإسلام" وله "فيض الخاطر" مـــجموع مقالات في سبعة مـــجلدات.

(١) الـــخريطة : ما ترسم عليه هيئة الأرض أو إقليم منها

(٢) جبس : الـــجص الذي يبنى به

(٣) الثكلى : التـــي فقد ولـــدها

(٤) الكحل : مصدر كحل من باب سمع يقال كحل الرجل أي كان أكحل العينين خلقة

الفرق بين الناس في الْحياة والناس على الشاشة[١] البيضاء؟ وهل تعرف الفرق بين الصوت والصدى[٢]؟ إن عرفتَ ذلك فهو بعينه الفرق بين الدين الحق والدين الصناعي.

يكدّ الباحثون أذهانَهم ، ويُجهد المؤرخون أنفسهم في تقليب صحفهم ووثائقهم عن تعرف السبب في أن الْمسلمين أول أمرهم أتوا بالعجائب، فغزوا وفتحوا وسادوا ، والْمسلمين في آخر أمرهم أتوا بالعجائب أيضا ، فضعفوا وذلوا واستكانوا ، والقرآن هو القرآن ، وتعاليم الإسلام هي تعاليم الإسلام ، ولآ إله إلا الله هي لآ إله إلا الله ، وكل شيء هي كل شيء ، ويذهبون في تعليل ذلك مذاهب شتى ، ويسلكون مسالك متعددة. ولا أرى لذلك إلا سببا واحدا وهو الفرق بين الدين الحق والدين الصناعي.

الدين الصناعي حركات وسكنات وألفاظ ولا شيء وراء ذلك ، و الدين الحق دين روح وقلب وحرارة. الصلاة في الدين الصناعي ألعاب رياضية، والحج حركة آلية ورحلة بدنية ، والمظاهر الدينية أعمال مسرحية أو أشكال بهلوانية.

---

(١) الشاشة : يريد الستار الذي يمثل القصة

(٢) الصدى : ما يرده الجبل أو غيره إلى الصوت مثل صوته ج أصداء

و "لآ إله إلا الله" في الدين الصناعي قول جميل لا مدلول له. أما في الدين الحق فهي كل شيء ، هي ثورة على عبادة المال ، وثورة على عبادة السلطان ، وثورة على عبادة الجاه ، وثورة على عبادة الشهوات ، وثورة علي كل معبود غير الله. "لآ إله إلا الله" في الدين الصناعي تتفق مع إحناء الرأس والْخُضوع لشهوة البدن ، وتتفق مع الذلة والْمسكنة، و "لآ إله إلا الله" في الدين الحق لا تتفق إلا مع الْحق. "لآ إله إلا الله" في الدين الصناعي تذهب مع الريح وفي الدين الْحق تزلزل الْجبال.

الدين الصناعي صناعة كصناعة النجارة والحياكة ، يمهر فيها الماهر بالحذق والمران، أما الدين الحق فروح وقلب وعقيدة، ليس عملا ولكن يبعث على كل عمل جليل وكل عمل نبيل[1].

الدين الحق "إكسير" يحل في الميت فيحيا ، وفي الضعيف فيقوي. هو حجر الفلاسفة تضعه على النحاس والفضة والرصاص فتكون ذهبا. هو العقيدة التي تأتي بالمعجزات فيقف العلم والتاريخ والفلسفة أمامها حائرة : بم تعلل ، وكيف تشرح.

هو الترياق الذي تتعاطى منه قليلا فيذهب بكل سموم الحياة. وهو العنصر الكيمياوي الذي تمزج به الشعائر الدينية فتطير بك إلى الله ، وتمزج به الأعمال الدنيوية فتذلل العقاب مهما صعبت ، وتصل بك إلى الغرض مهما لاقت.

---

(١) النبيل : الجليل والعظيم

هو الذي وجده كل من نَجح ، وهو الذي فقده كل من خاب. هو الكهرباء [١] الذي يتصل فيدور العجل ، وينقطع فلا حركة ولا عمل. هو الذي يَحل فِي الأوتار فتوقع ، وكانت قبل حبالا ، وفِي الصوت فيغنّي وكان قبل هواء.

الدين الْحق يَحمل صاحبه علَى أن يَحيا له ويُحارب له. والدين الصناعي يَحمل صاحبه على أن يَحيا به ، ويتاجر به ويَحتال به. الدين الْحق يَجعل صاحبه فوق كل سلطة وفوق كل سياسة. والدين الصناعي يَحمل صاحبه على أن يلوي الدين ليخدم السلطات ويَخدم الساسة. الدين الْحق قلب وقوة ، والدين الصناعي نَحو وصرف وإعراب وكلام وتأويل. الدين الْحق إمتزاج بالروح والدم وغضب للحق ونفور من الظلم وموت فِي تَحقيق العدل. والدين الصناعي عمامة كبيْرة وقباء يلمع وفرجية [٢] واسعة الأكمام.

"الشهادة" فِي الدين الْحق هي ما قال الله تعالَى : "إن اللهَ اشْتَرى مِنَ الْمُؤمِنِينَ أنْفُسَهم وَأموَالَهُمْ بِأنَّ لَهُمُ الْجَنَّة يُقَاتلُون فِي سَبيلِ الله فَيَقْتُلُون وَيُقْتَلُون". و"الشهادة" فِي الدين الصناعِي إعراب جُملة وتَخريج مَتن وتفسير شَرح وتوجيه حاشية وتصحيح قول مؤلف ورد الأعتراض عليه.

١- الكهرباء : قوة تتولد فِي بعض الأجسام بواسطة الحك أو الحرارة أو الإنفعالات الكيمياوية أي تبني الحان الغناء على موقعها وميزانها.

٢- فرجية : نوع من الأقبية

الدين الْحق تَحسين علاقة الإنسان بالله . وتَحسين علاقة الإنسـان بالإنسان لتَحسين علاقتهم جَميعا بالله. والدين الصناعِي تَحسين علاقـة صاحبه بالإنسان لاستدرار رزق أو كسب جاه أو تَحصيل مغنم أو دفـع مغرم. لقد صدق من قال: "إن هذا الدين لا يصلح آخره إلا بِما صلح به أوله" وهل كان أوله إلا دين روح ، وهل كان آخره إلا دين صناعة؟

جناية أهل كل دين أن يبتعدوا ــ كلما تقدم بِهم الزمان ــ عن روحـه ويَحتفظوا بشكله ، وأن يقبلوا الأوضاع ، ويعكسوا التقدير ، فلا يكـون للروح قيمة ، ويكون للشكل كل القيمة.

شأن "الإيمان" شأن العشق ، يَحول البرودة حرارة ، والْخمول نباهـة ، والرذيلة فضيلة ، والأثرة إيقارا.

والإيمان الْحق كالعصا السحرية ، لا تَمس شيئا إلا ألْهبته ، ولا جـامدا إلا أذابته ، ولا مواتا إلا أحيته.

من لِي بِمن يأخذ الدين الصناعي بكل ما فيه ، ويبيعِني ذرَّة من الديـن الْحق فِي أسْمى معانيه؟

ولِي كبد مقـروحة من يبيعـنِي بِهـا كبدا ليست بذات قروح [1]

١- قروح : الثقافـة

٣ - الكتب المفضلة عندي

عباس محمود العقاد
١٨٨٩ - ١٩٦٤

هذا موضوع جليل ، ولكن هل تعرف أنني أفضل قراءة كتب فلسفة الدين ، وكتب التاريخ الطبيعي ، وتراجم العظماء ، وكتب الشعر ؟

إنني أقرأ هذه الكتب وأعتقد أن العلاقة بينها متينة ، وإن كانت تفترق في الظاهر ، لأنها ترجع إلي توسيع أفق الحياة أمام الإنسان .. فكتب فلسفة الدين تبين إلى أي حد تمتد الحياة قبل الولادة وبعد الموت. وكتب التاريخ الطبيعي تبحث في أشكال الحياة المختلفة وأنواعها المتعددة ، و تراجم العظماء معرض لأصناف عالية من الحياة القوية البارزة ، والشعر هو ترجمان العواطف ، فإنني أفضل من الكتب كل ما له مساس بسر الحياة.

ولد الأستاذ عباس محمود العقاد بأسوان (مصر) سنة ١٨٨٩م ودرس في مدرسة أسوان الابتدائية، ثم الثانوية وكان نهما بالقراءة فتثقف بنفسه. كان العقاد مُحبا للعزلة ، كثير القراءة ، كثير الكتابة ، يكتب في كل موضوع وفي كل غرض. مُجيد الكتابة في الشخصيات وتحليلها، وله ما يزيد علي ستين مؤلفا في الأدب والنقد والتاريخ والفلسفة. وقد استن طريقة جديدة في كتابة التاريخ والسير بعبقرياته المعروفة. يمتاز العقاد بالعمق وسعة الدراسة والثقافة والتحليل العلمي.

وتسألني ما هو سر الحياة ، فأقول على الإجمال أنني أعتقد أن الحياة أعم من الكون ، وأن ما يرى جامدا من هذه الأكوان أو مجردا من الحياة إن هو في نظري إلا أداة لإظهار الحياة في لون من الألوان أو قوة من القوى .. والحياة شيء دائم أبدي أزلي ، لا بداية له ولا نهاية ..

فإذا كنت تستطيع أن تعرف سر الله عرفت سر الحياة ، ولكننا مطالبون بأن نحفظ لأنفسنا في هذا المحيط الذي لا نهاية له أوسع دائرة يمتد إليها شعورنا وإدراكنا. والكتب هي وسائل الوصول إلي هذه الغاية. وهي النوافذ التي تطل على حقائق الحياة ، ولا تغني النوافذ عن النظر.

ومن جهة أخرى فإن الكتب طعام الفكر ، وتوجد أطعمة لكل فكر كما توجد أطعمة لكل بنية ، ومن مزايا البنية القوية أنها تستخرج الغذاء لنفسها من كل طعام. وكذلك الإدراك القوي يستطيع أن يجد غذاء فكريا في كل موضوع. وعندي أن التحديد في اختيار الكتب إنما هو كالتحديد في اختيار الطعام. وكلاهُما لا يكون إلا لطفل في هذا الباب أو مريض ، فاقرأ ما شئت تستفد إذا كان لك فكر قادر أو معدة عقلية تستطيع أن تهضم ما يلقي فيها من الموضوعات .وإلا فاجعل القابلية حكما لك فيما تختار لأن الجسم في الغالب يغذيه ما تشتهيه.

ولا تغنِي الكتب عن تجارب الحياة ، ولا تغني التجارب عن الكتب، لأننا نحتاج إلي قسط من التجربة لكي نفهم حق الفهم ، أما أن التجارب لا تغني عن الكتب ، فذلك لأن الكتب هي تَجارب آلاف من السنين في مختلف الأمم والعصور ولا يمكن أن تبلغ تجربة الفرد الواحد أكثر من عشرات السنين ..

ولا أظن أن هناك كتبا مكررة لأخرى ، لأني أعتقد أن الفكرة الواحدة إذا تناولها ألف كتاب أصبحت ألف فكرة ، ولم تعد فكرة واحدة .. ولِهذا أتعمد أن أقرأ في موضوع الواحد أقوال كتاب عديدين ، وأشعر أن هذا أمتع وأنفع من قراءة الموضوعات المتعددة. فمثلا أقرأ في حياة نابليون أكثر من أقوال ثلاثين كاتبا وأنا واثق من أن كل نابليون من هؤلاء هو غير نابليون الذي وصف في كتب الآخرين.

أما تأثير كل من أنواع الكتب الثلاثة : العلمية ، والأدبية ، والفلسفية فهو أن الكتب العلمية تعلمنا الضبط والدقة وتفيدنا المعارف المحدودة التي يشترك فيها جميع الناس ، والكتب الأدبية توسع دائرة العطف والشعور ، وتكشف لنا عن الحياة والجمال ، والكتب الفلسفية تنبه البصيرة وملكة الإستقصاء وتتعدى بالقارئ من المعلوم إلي المَجهول ، وتنتقل به من الفروع إلي الأصول.

وكل من هذه الأنواع لازم لتثقيف الإنسان ، وتعريفه جوانب هذا العالَم الذي يعيش فيه. وأنا أفضلها على هذا الترتيب : الأدبية ، فالفلسفية ، فالعلمية.

ولا يستطيع القارئ أن يحصر مقدار الفائدة التي يجنيها من كتاب ، فرب كتاب يَجتهد في قراءته كل الإجتهاد ، ثم لا يَخرج منها بطائل ، ورب كتاب تتصفحه تصفحا ، ثُم يترك في نفسه أثرا عميقا يظهر في كل رأي من آرائه ، وكل اتّجاه من اتّجاهات ذهنه ، فأنت لا تعرف حق المْعرفة "الطريقة" التي يضمن الفائدة التامة من قراءة الكتب ، ولكن لعل أفضل ما يشار به ــ على الإجمال ــ هو ألا تكره نفسك على القراءة ، وأن تدع الكتاب في اللحظة التي تشعر فيها بالفتور والإستثقال.

أما مقياس الكتاب المفيد فانك تتبينه من كل ما يزيد معرفتك وقوتك على الإدراك والعمل وتذوق الحياة ، فإذا وجدت ذلك في كتاب ما ، كان جديرا بالعناية والتقدير ، فإننا لا نعرف إلا لنعمل أو لنشعر ، أما المعرفة التي لا عمل وراءها ولا شعور فيها فخير منها عدمها. وعلى هذا المقياس تستطيع أن تفرق بين ما يصلح للثقافة والتهذيب وما لا يصلح.

٤ - قِوام الفُنــون

إبراهيم عبد القــادر المازني
١٨٨٩ - ١٩٤٩

الأدبُ إلْهامٌ وفنٌّ ، ولكلِّ فنٍّ أدواتُه وآلاتُه ، ولا بدَّ فيه من الإحسان والتجويد ، أي من الصَّبْر ، وصِحَّة النظر ، وسلامة الذوق ، وصدق السريرة [١] وحسن الإستعداد.

وما كان الصوابُ وصحةُ النظر ودقة الإحساس وحسنُ التَّخيُّل والقدرة على ذلك وغيره بمقصورة على الأدباء ، ولا هي بوقف عليهم ، ولكنْ كمْ مِمن تفيضُ وخواطرهم بالْخيالات[٢] الرائعة والآراء السديدة [٣] والإحساسات العميقة يستطيعون أن يُبرزوا هذه ، وتُحدثوا

ولد الْمازِني في القاهرة سنة ١٨٨٩م وتبين للدارس أن الْمازِني عندما أكمل دروسه الثانوية قد حاول أن يدرس الطب فلم يرق له وشاء أن يتعلم الهندسة فلم يتوفر لديه المال اللازم لذلك ومِما لا شك فيه بأن المازِني ترك للأجيال العربية كثيرا من النثر والشعر – يصور الحياة كما يراها من خلال تَجاربه الشخصية ومن أجواء بيته وحياته – وقصص الْمازِني بصورة عامة مستوحاة من اختباراته الشخصية أو من وقائع الحياة التي عرفها – وهي في الْحقيقة مرآة صادقة تعكس بدقة الْمجتمع المصري كما تراءى للمازِني بِحسناته وسيئاته – بتطوره وجُموده.

(١) السريرة : ما يسره الإنسان من أمره ، والنية.

(٢) الخيالاِت : يقصد بِها الأخيلة جمع خيال.

(٣) الآراء السديدة : السديد القاصد إلى الحق والرأي السديد المستقيم

فيها صورا ، ويَجلوها كما هي في نفوسهم؟ الألفاظ التـــي هي أدواتُ الكتابة موجودة ، ولعـــلَّ غيـــر الأديب لها أحفظ ، وبِها أعلم وهـــي في طريق من شاء ، غيـــر أنَّها ليست كل ما يَحتاجُ إليه الْمرء ، ليكون منه كاتب.

كذلك الأصباغُ والألوان حاضرة ، من شاء مَدَّ إليها يده ، وتناولَـــها ، وصنع بِها ما أحبَّ ، وهي مادة التصوير ، ولكن من الذي يَحْسَب أنَّـها كل ما ينقصُ الْمرء ليكون مصوراً؟

وكذلك لا يُغنـــي العلمُ بالقواعد والأصول ، وما عسى أن تكون قيمتها وحدها؟ هذا وجهٌ يريد المصورُ أن يرسُـــمه ، ويَنقـــل إلى اللـــوح مـــا يترقرق[1] في صفحته من الْمعانِي ، ويجولُ فيه من الأمواه [2] ، فكيـــف ذلك؟

كيف يَجعل هذه الشفَة ناطقة بالسُّخريـــة ، أو تقوية الذقن مُعبِّرة عـــن التصميم أو لَمعة العين شاهدة بسجاحة الْخلق [3] ورِضا النفس؟

---

(١) يترقرق : تظهر فيه

(٢) الأمواه : جَمع ماء

(٣) سَجاحة الخلق : سهولة الخلق ولينه

كيف يُشعرك بِما يشعر هو به من السِّحر أو الدلال أو القوة أو الجلال [١] ويفيدك ما أفاد من الأنس والغبطة [٢] والروح؟

أو كيف يَجعلُك حين تنظر إلى الصورة الْحاكية [٣] تشتهي ــ مثله حين يَجتلي الأصل [٤] ــ أن تُغمض عينيك ، وتنقل نفسك إلى عالم آخر من الخيالات والْخواطر والإحساسات ، وما يقال عن المصور يقال مثله أو أكثر منه عن الكاتب أو الشاعر.

والأمر فِي كلتا الْحالتين يَحتاج إلى فطرةٍ مُهيأةٍ له أسبابُها ، وذوق مؤازر [٥] وسليقة [٦] مُناصرة ، وملَكة مُعِينة على حسن اختيار الرموز الكفيلة بإفراغ الْخواطر في القوالب الْملائمة ، والقادرة على إحداث الصور المطلوبة في أذهان القرَّاء ، وعلى ذلك يكون صانعا لا أكثر مَن مارس الفنَّ وحُرِم الإلْهام - صانعا كهذه الآلات التي تدور بلا روح ، وتُخرج ألوانا وضُروبا من الصور تُعجب بصقلها ودقِّتِها وإحكام صيغتها ، ولا تُحسُّ أن يد إنسان حيٍّ أو قلبه وراءها.

---

(١) الجلال : العظمة والسمو

(٢) الغبطة والروح : المسرة وحسن الحال، والروح : الراحة

(٣) الحاكية : التي تحكي الأصل وتمثله

(٤) يجتلي : ينظر إليه ويتبينه بجلاء

(٥) مؤازر : والمراد أن الفن يحتاج إلي طبع وذوق معا

(٦) السليقة : الطبيعة والفطرة

٥ ـ ألف ليلة وليلة

الأستاذ أحمد حسن الزيات
١٨٨٥ ـ ١٩٦٩

إن من يطلب من ألف ليلة وليلة فلسفة خاصة ، وفكرة عامة ، ووجهة مشتركة كان كمن يطلب من كافة الناس عقيدة واحدة ، وطبيعة ثابتة ، وأغراضا متفقة ، فهو كتاب شعبي يصور الحياة الدنيا كما هي لا كما ينبغي أن تكون ، فإذا رأينا مذاهبه تتناقض ، ومراميه تتعارض ، وآراءه تَختلف ، فذلك لأن المجتمع الذي يصوره كذلك.

ولَم يكن الكتاب نتاج قريِحة معلومة ، ولا نتيجة خطة مرسومة ، حتى نتلمس في جوانبه الدوافع والنوازع والغاية ، إن هو إلا صدى يتردد

ولد أحْمد حسن الزيات في عام ١٨٨٥م في إحدى ضواحي القاهرة وانتقل إلي القاهرة والتحق بالجامع الأزهر وتلقى العلوم الأزهرية علي أساتذته من أساطين العلم منهم السيد علي المرصفي والشيخ محمد عبده. والتحق بالْجامعة الْمصرية القديْمة وتلقي تاريخ الأدب العربِي والفرنسي علي المستشرقيْن الإيطاليين "كويوي" و "فريننوو" ودرس الحقوق وأتَم تعليمه العالي للحقوق في جامعة باريس، وعاد وتقلب في وظائف تدريس الأدب العربي في القاهرة وبغداد حتى استقر بالقاهرة. وأصدر سنة ١٩٣٣م مجلة "الرسالة" التي بقيت تَخدم الأدب العربي عشرين سنة كانت فيها ملتقي الكتاب النابغين ومدرسة الأدباء الناشئين وتولى رئاسة تحرير مجلة الأزهر . ومات في ١٩٦٩م.

خافتاً لعقائد الشرق القديْم وعقلياته وعاداته. فــفي الفلسفة نراه يتأثر بالأفلاطونية الحديثة ، والأخلاق الإسلامية ، فيدعو إلي القناعة باليسير، والعزوف عن الدنيا ، والاعتدال في اللذة ، والمبالغة في الحــذر ، والتفويض المطلق للقدر ، فروحه ، من هذه الجهة ، تتنافر مع صــورة البــراقة ، ووسائله الطماحة، وحوادثه المغامرة. ثُم نراه في أقــاصيص أخرى ولا سيما الحديثة يزين الأنانية ، ويرتضي القسوة ، ويتشــوف إلى المكاسب الدنيئة ، ويشرَه إلي اللذة الجنسية ، ولا يكاد يعتقد بــالعواطف الكريْمة. وقد يصور الْمتاع الحسّي ، واللهو الجموح بِمــا لا يَتمثــل في الذهن إلا على سبيل الخيال ، كالذي يحكيه عن فتــى من أبناء الملــوك أرسى إلي جزيرة كلٌّ من فيها تُجار وصناع نساءٌ كأنّهن اللؤلؤ المكنــون ، فقضى بينهن في هذا النعيم أياماً أقل ما أصاب فيها من اللذه أنــه كــان يلقي الشبكة في الماء علي سبيل اللهو ، فتخرج إليه من الأصداف خريدة من بنات الجان ، كانّها حورية من حور الجنان ، إلخ.. فإذا اختبرنــاه في السياسة والاجتماع رأيناه مَلَكيا يقيم في كل مدينة عرشــاً ، وينصــب علي كل مَجمع من الأحياء ملكاً ، حتــى الحيات والحشرات والطيــور والوحوش والقردة ؛ دِيمقراطيا يشترك الملك والصعلوك في مُتَع الحيــاة ومَجالي الأنس ؛ عائليا يبنــي نظام البيت وتأثيل الَمجد علــى الزوجــة والولد ، لذلك تَجدونه يستهل معظم أقاصيصه بِحنين الوالديــن إلي النسل ، وفزعهما إلي الله أو إلي الْمنجّم من داء العقم. وقد يسمو مغزاه

إلي الفلسفة الاجتماعية العالية ، مثال ذلك حكاية السندباد والحمّال . فالحمَال يؤدُّه الحِمل الفادح ، وينهكه الحر اللافح ، فيلقي حَمله علي مصطبة أمام بيت من بيوت التجار يتردد إليه النسيم الرطيب ، وتضُوع منه روائح العطر والطيب ، ثُم يرى عظمة ذلك التاجر في كثرة خدمه وغلمانه ، ويسمع تغريد البلابل والفواخت في بستانه ، ويصغي إلي رنين أوتاره وغناه قيانه ، وينْشقُّ أفاويه الطعام الشهي من صحافه وألوانه، فيرفع طرفه الحائر إلي السماء ويقول : سبحانك يا رب! لا اعتراض علي حكمك ولا معقب لأمرك! أين حالي من حال هذا التاجر؟ أنا مثله وهو مثلي ، ولكن حَمله غير حَملي!

٦ - أدب الجاحظ

محمد كرد علي
١٨٧٦ - ١٩٥٣

يطالعك الْجاحظ من بارع أدبه بالإبداع دونه كل إبداع ، ويعلّمك في سهولة ويسر لا يشق عليك ، يدخل من نفسك مدخل صدق ، ويستهويك وأنت لا تدري كيف أخذت. قد تقرأ لغيره كلاماً ، وتُعجَب بِما فيه من ديباجة حسنة أو معنى دقيق ، أو تَحقيق وإحاطة ، أو فكر طريف ، أو رأي نادر ، أما أن يضمّ الكلام شتيت هذه الميزات ، ويَحمل كل ما يعنّ للخاطر من الصفات ، فهذا مِما لا يقع إلا على الندرة في كلام البلغاء ، وهو من الأمور المعتادة في كلام أَبِي عثمان . أنت تتمثل فيما يُملي الكاتبون شيئا تستطيبه وتستملحه ، وفي أدبه كل ما يُطرب ويُعجب. الكتّاب في العادة يتطالون إلي أن يكتبوا موضوعاتهم ، والجاحظ يستمليه موضوعه فيمليه ، لا يتكلف ولا يتعسف. يصور لك

محمد كرد علي ولد في سوريا سنة ١٨٧٦م وكتب وهو في السادسة عشر من عمره وحرّر أول جريدة ظهرت في دمشق وكتب في مجلة "المقتطف" وبذلك امتدت شهرته. وفي سنة ١٩١٩م اقترح إنشاء مجمع علمي عربي واختير أول رئيس له كان الأستاذ محمد كرد علي صحفيا ومنشئا مترسلا بعمل الثقافة العربية الجديدة والثقافة العربية القديمة. يمتاز أسلوبه بالرقة من غير تفخيم وسهولة في التعبير من غير تكليف ويرسل النفس على سجيتها. ومن أعظم كتبه "خطط الشام" في ستة أجزاء واسعة و"الإسلام والحضارة العربية" في جزءين.

خلجات الروح ، وآهات النفس ، وأزمات العقل ، ويرسم لك المحسوسات كأنك تَحسها، ويصف لك المعلوم والمْجهول، ويعرض عليك المعقول والمنقول ، ويفيض كل الفيض بِما لم يكتب لغير أفراد في علماء هذه الأمة الطويلُ تاريْخُها ، الكثير نبغاوها ؛ كأن الجاحظ بوق عصره ومصره ، والآلة المحكمة التي أحسنت نقل أصوات أهل جيله. سجّل المفاخر والمعاير ، وحَمل إلى أبناء القرون اللأحقة أفانين من أدبه جَمَّلها بروح الحق وسحر الجمال.

يقف القارئ بِما ينقل إليه على صور رآها بعينه ، فأحب إمتاع غيره برؤيتها ، وإشراكه بِحالات تأثرت بها نفسه ، وهو مِمن ربط ماضي الأمة بِمستقبلها ، ودينها بدنياها ، وتعمّد لفرط أمانته أن يسمعها الحسن والقبيح ، فطبَّ بلطف عبقريته روحها وجسمها . وإذا كنت مِمن لا يتوقع من المصور أكثر من أن يصور لك ما يقع بصره عليه، فأدب الجاحظ يصور لك في حذق وتدقيق ما وقعت عليه عينه وقلبه و حسه. ولِما كان من رقة الشعور إلى التي ليس بعدها ، جاء كلام شعورا وعاطفة.

ينبعث البهاء في أدب الجاحظ من كون مادة الجمال فيه سيَّالة ، براقة ، ناصعة ، تنشر السرور في الروح., قالوا: إذا أورثك الكلام ما يعلو به فكرك ، وما ينبّه فيك حسا شريفاً ، فلا تبحثن بعدها عن شيء آخر

لتحكم علي ما قرأت ، وكن على مثل اليقين أنه من الجيد الصالِح ، وأنه ما صدر إلا عن يد صناع ، وقريْحة وقادة. والْجاحظ فوق هذا لم يتقيد كثيرا بذوق عصره ، وفي ذلك إبداعه في أدبه.

كتب بعد الدرس الطويل والخبرة الواسعة ، وما عانَى من الأبحاث إلا ما اضطلع به، وما قولك بعظيم يحيط بأكثر ما في صحيفة الوجود من المعارف، ويعرف ما في الأرض من تعاجيب ، وما في السماء من غرائب، ووكده مصروف إلى إرضاء من يواصل السير معه، ويرافقه ويعاشره من قرَّائه. ومن لا يَحتقر شيئا يدخل في باب الآداب ، ولا يستنكف من الأخذ عن صغير الناس وكبيرهم، ويكشف كل غامض، ويستقري ويستنبط، خليق أن يفعل أدبه في النفوس، وأن يكون كلامه راحا للأرواح.

قيل إن الكتابة الصحيحة صعبة المرأس ، وأصعب منها اختراع تركيب جديد ، وإن جودة الكتابة تتوقف علي استبطان أسرار الأشياء، ومنها أي يسلي الكاتب السامع بالمناظر المختلفة ، يَجمع له منها أصنافا، وينقله في الأحاسيس، ويبعد به عن المهجورات والْمكررات، ويهيب به إلَى الإشراف على ما تَخترع قريْحته، ويتكشف عنه بيانه. وهذا القول يصدق على الْجاحظ إذا تأملت تراكيبه، وبصره بالأشياء ، حتّى لا يترك قولا لغيره إذا بدا له أن يقوله.

فصلان للجاحظ أبدع فيهما الإبداع كله : أحدهما في وصف الكتاب والثاني في وصف الحسد. ولعل إجادة الجاحظ تَجلَّت لنا فيهما لأن موضوعهما مِما أهمه كثيرا. ومَن أعرف بنفع الكتب من سيد من صنفها ، ومَن أقدر على وصف الحسد ، من العارف بِمدب هذا الداء من نفوس الحساد ، ومن كل طول حياته غرضا لَهم يُحاولون أن يصيبوه فيتقيهم. إنتقد بعضهم على الجاحظ حتى وضعه الكتب ، فذكر لَهم فضلها على الناس ، ومِما قال : الإنسان لا يعلم حتى يكثر سماعه ، ولا بد أن تكون كتبه أكثر من سماعه ، ولا يعلم ولا يَجمع العلم حتى يكون الإنفاق عليه من ماله ألذّ عنده من الإنفاق من مال عدوه ، ومن لم تكن نفقته التي تَخرج في الكتب ألذّ عنده من عِشق القيان ، لم يبلغ في العلم مبلغا رضيًّا ، وليس ينتفع بإنفاقه حتى يؤثر اتّخاذ الكتب إيثار الأعرابي فرسه باللبن علي عياله ، وحتّى يؤمّل في العلم ما يؤمل الأعرابي في فرسه.

ولا بد من الإشارة أخيرا إلي أن الجاحظ كان صريحا في أدبه ، لا يبالي تشدد المتزمتين ، يسمى الأشياء بأسمائها ، رغم أنف من رضي وكره ، فأدبه الأدب الواقع على ما يدعوه المعاصرون ، أي نقل الطبيعة كما هي، أو كما يظن أن تُرى ، مع ما فيها من بشاعة وابتذال.

٧ - علمتني الحياة

الدكتورة سهير قلماوي

الْحياة تعلمنا كل يوم درسا ، لو أننا استطعنا أن نطيل التامل في كل ما يحدث لنا .. والعجيب أننا نتلقى فيها دروسا أحيانا من قوم يفترض أننا نَحن الذين نلقنهم الدروس ، فكم من درس علمه إياي طلابِي ، بل كم من درس علمه إياي ابنِي! ولقد فكرت مرارا فِي أن أخرج كتيبا صغيرا بعنوان "علمنِي ابنِي " فان تَجربة الأمومة مَملوءة بِهذه المواقف التِي يعلو فيها حس الطفل البرئ إلي مستوى أرقى من حس الإنسان الكبير ، بفضل صفاء الذهن حينا ، أو بفضل عدم تراكم المؤثرات عليه ، وهاك درسا علمه إياي ابنِي :

كنت وأنا صغيرة أعجب كثيرا بقصيدة فرنسية تعلمتها في نَحو العاشرة وحفظت أبياتَها عن ظهر قلب عنوانِها "الْحمار والضفدعة " وفيها يصف الشاعر الواعظ كيف أن صبيين يلعبان بالطوب و الحصي في الشارع قد وجدوا ضفدعة ، فجمعا قدرا من الحصي ، ووقفا في

إحدى أديبات مصر المشهورات في العصر الحديث كانت أول طالبة نالت شهادة الدكتورة في الأدب من الجامعة المصرية، وهي تَمتاز بحسن إطلاعها على الأدب القديْم والآداب الأجنبية المعاصرة.

مكان يسمح لَهما بتسديد الْحصي إليها ، وفي هذه اللحظة مر حِمار مجهد يَجر عربة ، وكاد أن يدوس الضفدعة برجله ، وفَجأة يقف وينحاز جانبا حتى لا يدوسها ، وينظر الصبيان إلَي الْحمار وقد تناثر من أيديهما الطوب والحصي ، ويقول الأول في خجل لرفيقه "ماذا كنا نفعل يا رفيقي؟ إن الحمار أقل شرا منا"!

وأخذت أشرح القصيدة لابنِي ، وأحاول أن أبين له أن عادة إلقاء الطوب والأحجار على المارة قد تؤدي إلى أخطار جسيمة. ولكن ابنِي لاحظ أننِي أسترسل في الوعظ والإرشاد وهو ينفر من هذا كل النفور. فسألنِي كمن يريد تغيير الموضوع "هل توجد الضفادع في الشوارع إننِي لم أرها ..؟" فشرحت له أن الشاعر يتحدث عن شارع في قرية ، وبينت له الفرق الذي أقنعه آخر الأمر إلي حد ما أن الشاعر على حق ، ولكنه يلتفت إليّ وعلى وجهه الحلو بسمة بسخرية قائلا : هذا كلام ، مجرد كلام! الحمار الذي يضرب به المثل في الغباء هو الذي يدرك أنه يسحق ضفدعة وهو الذي يشفق عليها؟ كلام ، مجرد كلام. الحمار الحمار"

وتلقنت الدرس الْمهول من ابنِي. إن الفرق بينِي وبينه هو أنِّي كنت أعيش في عصر يعرف قيمة الْمجاز ويبهر بسحر الإستعارة ويُحب أن يَخدعه الشاعر مادام سيصل بذلك في النهاية إلي أن يرفع من روحه

ويرقق من حسه. أما ابنِي فإنه يعيش "لسوء الْحظ" في عصر آخر ، عصر لا يريد إلا أن يعرف الحقائق المُجردة ، وكدت أسترسل معه لأسأله : وهل هناك حقيقة مُجردة يا بنَي..؟ وأين الحقيقة ؟ ولكنِّي رأيته بَرماً قلقا يريد ان يَجرى ليلعب مع إخوانه فتركته، ولكنّي أدركت منذ ذلك اليوم عمق تلك الْهُوَّة السحيقة التِي يُمكن أن تفصل بين جيلين ، والتِي لا بد للجيل القديم من أن يدركها ليعمل على ملئها وإنشاء الجسور عليها ، حتّى لا يهيم جيل جديد في مهامه المادة بلا روح ، وتعلمت من ابنِي درسا لم أنسه إلي اليوم.

٨ - مستقبل اللغة العـربية

جبران خليل جبران
١٨٨٣ - ١٩٣١

إنّما اللغة مظهر من مظاهر الإبتكار فِي مَجموع الأمة ، أو ذاتِها العامـة، فإذا هجعت قوة الإبتكار توقفت اللغة عن مسيْرها، وفِي الوقوف التقهقر وفِي التقهقر الموت واندثار.

إذن فمستقبل اللغة العربية يتوقف على مستقبل الفكر المبدع الكائن - أو غيْر الكائن - فِي مَجموع الأقطار التِي تتكلم اللغة العربيـة. فإن كـان ذلك الفكر موجودا كان مستقبل اللغة عظيما كماضيها ، وإن كان غـيْر موجود فمستقبلها سيكون كحاضر شقيقتيها السريانية والعبـرانية.

١- ففي الجاهلية كان الشاعر يتأهب لأن العرب كانوا في حالة التأهب. وكان ينمو ويتمدد أيام الْمخضرمين لأن العرب كانوا في حالـة النمو

أشهر كتاب لبنان في الثلث الأول من القرن العشرين. أديب ومصور وشاعر ورائد من رواد النهضة الحديثة. ولد جبران خليل جبران في بشرَى ١٨٨٣م (لبنـان) وهاجر طفلا إلي بوسطن من بلدان الولايات المتحدة حيث درس فـن التصوير وتضلع في اللغة الإنجليزية. ثُم عاد إلي لبنان فدرس العربية ورجع بعدها إلي المـهجر وظل فيه حتّى توفي عام ١٩٣١م. يَمتاز اسلوبه بسعة الخيال وروعـة التصوير وعذوبة الموسيقي إلي جانب ما يتضمنه من أفكار جديدة متمردة.

والتمدد. وكان يتشعب أيام المولدين لأن الأمة الإسلامية كانت فِي حالة التشعب. وظل الشاعر يتدرج ويتصاعد ويتلون فيظهر آناً كفيلسوف، و آونة كطبيب، وأخرى كفلكي، حتّى راود النعاس قوة الإبتكار فِي اللغة العربية فنامت ، وبنومها تَحول الشعراء إلي ناظمين والفلاسفة إلي كلاميين والأطباء إلي دجالين والفلكيون إلي منجمين.

إذا صحّ ما تقدم كان مستقبل اللغة العربية رهْنَ قوة الإبتكار في مَجموع الأقطار التِي تتكلمها ، فإن كان لتلك الأقطار ذات خاصة أو وحدة معنوية وكانت قوة الإتبكار في تلك الذات قد استيقظت بعد نومها الطويل كان مستقبل اللغة العربية عظيما كماضيها ، وإلا فلا.

٢- وما عسى أن يكون تأثير التمدين الأوروبِي والروح الغربية فيها ؟ إنّما التأثير شكل من الطعام تتناوله اللغة من خارجها ، فتمضغه وتبتلعه ، وتحول الصالح منه إلي كيانِها الْحي كما تحول الشجرة النور والهواء وعناصر التراب إلى أفنان فأوراق فأزهار فأثْمار . ولكن إذا كانت اللغة بدون أضراس تقضم ولا معدة تَهضم، فالطعام يذهب سدى، بل ينقلب سُمُا قاتلا.

وأما الروح الغربية فهي دور من أدوار الإنسان وفصل من فصول حياته. وحياة الإنسان موكب هائل يسيْر دائما إلي الأمام ، ومن ذلك الغبار

الذهبِي الْمتصاعد من جوانب طريقه تتكون اللغات والحكومات والمذاهب. فالأمم التِي تسيْر في مقدمة هذا الموكب هي المبتكرة ، والْمبتكر مؤثر ، والأمم التِي تَمشي في مؤخرته هي الْمقلدة ، والْمقلد يتأثر، فلما كان الشرقيون سابقين والغربيون لاحقين كان لِمدنيتنا التأثيْر العظيم فِي لغاتِهم ، وها قد أصبحوا هم السابقين ، وأمسينا نَحن اللاحقين، فصارت مدنيتهم - بِحكم الطبع - ذات تأثيْر عظيم في لغتنا وأفكارنا وأخلاقنا.

بيد أن الغربيين كانوا في الماضي يتناولون ما نطبخه ، فيمضغون ويبتلعونه مُحولين الصالح منه إلي كيانِهم الغربِي ، أما الشرقيون في الوقت الْحاضر فيتناولون ما يطبخه الغربيون ويبتلعونه ، ولكنه لا يتحول إلَي كيانِهم ، بل يُحولُهم إلى شبه غربيين ، وهي حالة أخشاها وأتبرم منها!

إن روح الغرب صديق وعدو لنا ، صديق إذا تَمكنا منه ، وعدوّ إذا تَمكن منا. صديق إذا فتحنا له قلوبنا ، وعدوّ إذا وهبنا له قلوبنا. صديق إذا أخذنا منه ما يوافقنا ، وعدوّ إذا وضعنا نفوسنا في الحالة التِي توافقه.

٣- وما يكون تأثير التطور السياسي الحاضر في الأقطار العربية ؟

قد أجمع الكتاب المفكرون في الغرب والشرق على أن الأقطار العربية في حالة من التشويش السياسي والإداري والنفسي ، ولقد اتفق أكثرهم على أن التشويش مجلبة الخراب والإضمحلال.

أما أنا فأسأل : هل هو تشويش أم ملل؟ إن كان مللاً فالْملل نِهاية كل أمة وخاتِمة كل شعب ، الملل هو الإحتضار في صورة النعاس ، والموت في شكل النوم.

وإن كان بالْحقيقة تشويشا فالتشويش في شرعي ينفع دائما ، لأنه يبين ما كان خافيا في روح الأمة ، ويبدل نشوتَها بالصحو ، وغيبوبتها باليقظة ، ونظيْر عاصفة تَهز بعزمها الأشجار لا لتقلعها ، بل لتكسر أغصانَها اليابسة وتبعثر أوراقها الصفراء. وإذا ما ظهر التشويش فِي أمة لم تزل علي شيء من الفطرة فهو أوضح دليل على وجود قوة الإتبكار في أفرادها والإستعداد في مَجموعها.

إذن فتأثيْر التطور السياسي سيحوِّل ما في الأقطار العربية من التشويش إلي نظام، وما في داخلها من الغموض والإشكال إلي ترتيب وألفة ، ولكنه لا ولن يبدل مللها بالوجد وضجرها بالحماسة.

٤- هل يعمّ انتشار اللغة العربية في المدارس العالية وغيْر العالية وتُعلّم بِها جَميع العلوم ؟

لا يعمُّ انتشار اللغة في المدارس العالية وغيْر العالية حتّى تصبح تلك المدارس ذات صبغة وطنية مُجردة ، ولن تعلم بِها جَميع العلوم حتّى

تنتقل الْمدارس من أيدي الْجمعيات الْخيْرية واللجان الطائفية و البعثات الدينية إلي أيدي الْحكومات المحلية.

ففي سوريا ـ مثلا ـ كان التعليم يأتينا من الغرب بشكل الصدقة ، وقد كنا ولم نزل نلتهم خبز الصدقة لأننا جياع متضوِّرون ، ولقد أحيانا ذلك الخبز ولما أحيانا أماتنا. أحيانا لأنه أيقظ جَميع مداركنا ونبه عقولنا قليلا، وأماتنا لأنه فرّق كلمتنا وأضعف وحدتنا وقطع روابطنا وأبعد ما بين طوائفنا ، حتَى أصبحت بلادنا مَجموعة مستعمرات صغيرة ، مُختلفة الأذواق ، متضاربة المشارب ، كل مستعمرة منها تشد في حبل إحدى الأمم الغربية ، وترفع لواءها ، وتترنّم بِمحاسنها وأمْجادها.

وقد يكون ميلنا السياسي إلي الأمة التِي نتعلم علي نفقتها دليلا على عاطفة عرفان الجميل في نفوس الشرقيين ، ولكن ما هذه العاطفة التِي تبنِي حجرا من جهة واحدة وتَهدم جدارا من الجهة الأخرى؟ما هذه العاطفة التِي تستنبت زهرة وتقتلع غابة؟ ما هذه العاطفة التِي تُحيينا يوما وتُميتنا دهرا ؟

نعم سوف يعم إنتشار اللغة العربية في المدارس العالية وغير العالية وتعلم بِها جميع العلوم ، فتتوحَّد ميولنا السياسية ، وتتبلور منازعنا القومية ، لأنه في المدرسة تتوحد الميول ، وفي المدرسة تتجوهر الْمنازع ، ولكن لا

يتم هذا حتّى يصيْر بإمكاننا تعليم الناشئة علي نفقة الأمة. لا يتم هـــذا حتّى يصير الواحد منا إبنا لوطن واحد بدلا من وطنين متناقضين أحدهمـا لِجسده والآخر لروحه ، لا يتــم هذا حتى نستبدل خبز الصدقة بِخـــبز معجون في بيتنا ، لأن المتسوِّل الْمحتاج لا يستطيع أن يشـــترط علـى المتصدق الأريْحي. ومن يضع نفسه في منْزلة الموهوب لا يستطيع معارضة الواهب ، فالْموهوب مسيّر دائِما والواهب مُخيّر أبدا.

أدب الْمهجر وأهم خصائصهه : يُراد بأدب المهجر أدب العرب الذين هاجروا مـن بلاد الشام إلَى أمريكا الشمالية والجنوبية، وكوّنوا فيها جاليات عربية، كــان لهـا نشاط أدبِي متعدد الْمظاهر.

ويُمكن إجْمال المؤثرات التي وجهت أدبُهم فيما يلي:

١- تفاعل شخصيتهم الشرقية مع الغرب الجديد الذي نزحوا إليه وعاشوا فيها.

٢- الإتصال الوثيق بالثقافات الأجنبية التِي عاشوا فِـــي أجوائـــها وبالأدبـاء والْمنتديات الأدبية الأمريكية وإتجاهات الأدب الأمريكي ونزعاته وبخاصـــة النزعة الروحية والتأملية التي كانت غالبة على كتاب الجيل الْماضِي.

٣- تطلّع المهاجرين إلَى وطنِهم الأول وحنينهم الدائِم إليه.

٤- تَمسكهم بقوميتهم العربية مِما دفعهم إلي تتبع الأحداث بـــالوطن العـــربي وشغف والمشاركة ـــ علي البعد ـــ فِي كل ما يَجري به، واعتزازهم بأمْجـــاد جدودهم وبقديْم التراث الحضاري لوطنهم العربي الذي ينتمون إليه. وأهـــم خصائص أدب المهجر هي: (١) النزعة الإنسانية (٢) النزعة الروحية.

٩ ـ نور الأندلس

أمين الريحـــاني
١٨٧٦ ـ ١٩٤٠

من حسنات الْحياة زيارة الأندلس ، ومن الكفارات عن ذنوب النـــاطق بالضاد ، الحج إلَى الْحمراء التِي قال فيها الشاعر :

تَمد لــها الجوزَاءُ [١] كف مصافح ويدنو لَها بــدرُ الســماء مناجيــا

ومن حظي أنّي كنت من الحاجين ، زرت البِلادَ الْمباركـــة ، وتنشــقت هواءَها ، وسَمعت أهلها يناجون السرور ليلَ نَهار بعيونِهم و بأرواحهم الخفيفة ، ساعة اللهو والطرب. ومن غريب الأمور أن فِي قلب الأندلس ملجأ قلما يلجأ أليه الأندلسيون ، فهناك مقامٌ لا تُسمع فيه ضجـــة ، ولا تصل إليه أصداء ، مقامٌ بل مقاماتٌ هي أجْملُ مـــا في الأندلـــس أثــرا وذكرا، وقد كان لَها من السرور أيامٌ زاهرة ، ومن الطرب ليل بـــاهرة عاطرةٌ ، ومن الْمجد أعلام وقبابٌ ، ومعـــاهدُ وأنصاب [٢] ما تبقي منها

أمين الريحاني كاتب ورحالة ولد في الفريكة (لبنـــان) إنتقل إلَى الولايات المتحـــدة صغيرا. عـــاد إلَى لبنان وأقام في قرية شهوان يتعلم العربيـــة وآدابـــها، ويعلـــم الإنكليزية ، ثُم عاد إلَى أمريكا وأخذ يكتب بالعربيـــة والإنكليزية فِـــي الأدب والنقد والإجْتماع والسياسة وقد اشتهر بدعوته إلَي التوفيق بين حضارتَي الشـــرق والغرب ومناهضته الحكم الأجنبي في البلاد العربية.

(١) الجوزاء : برج من أبراج السماء

(٢) أنصاب / أعلام منصوبة

اليوم غيـــر طلول [١] متهدمة نبتت في جدرانِها الأعشـــاب ، و نظـــم العنكبوتُ مرثاته فوق النوافذ منها والأبواب ، وجلس في عروشها العالية السكون ، ودفن فِي جناتِها المهجورة الشعر والأدبُ والفنون...... طلول كانت بالأمس معاهدَ وقصورا هي دائرةُ الْمجد وقطبُ الحبـــور [٢] ، في قناطرها وقبابِها وأبوابِها، صناعة نادرة دقيقة وفي كل رسم من رســومها آية جَمال تُدهش حتَى اليوم أربابَ الفن ، وفي كل بيت من الشعر علـي جدرانِها درة من المعنَى أو زهرةٌ من التقوى منقوشة في بـــلاط منقطـــع النظير ، لوناً وتذهيباً. هذي آثارُ العرب ، وقد أمست عروشا للنسيان ، ومدفنا لِمجد الآباء والأجداد ، وظلالا تَجلب الأحزان ، وعبرة بليغـــة للإنسان ، وهي رغمَ ذلك بَهجةٌ للناظرين ، ومصدرُ وحـــي للشـــعراء الْمتفننيـــن.

ولكن الذكرى...... لله من ذكرى تقبض على النفس فتجعلها كالجمـــاد، لله من ذكريات وآثار تبْتهج لمرآها العين، فيذوب لِمعناها الفؤاد!! لله مـن مَجدكم وعزكم ابن أمية وابن عباد وعبد الرحْمن والمنصور والمعتمد[٣]

---

(١) طلول : ما تبقي من آثار

(٢) الْحبور : اصل السعادة والبهجة

(٣) الُمعتمد : رواد النهضة في العصر الأندلسي وعنهم أخذ الغرب أكثر علومه.

من شادوا معاهد العلم والدين ...... طالما اهتزت النفس لذكر مـآثركم ، وطالما وقفت العين شفقاً [١] عند اسْمائكم في التاريخ.

وتركت ما فِي أشبيلية من آثار وذكريات ، لأصل غرناطة قاعدة الدنيـــا في ذلك الزمان ، وحاضرةَ السلطان ومنها إلَى قرطبة مسقط رأس أبِــي الوليد ابن رشد ، لأشاهد الجامعَ الكبير الذي أصبح كنيسة قائِمة علـــى عمد الجامع القديْم ، ولأدخل بيوتا فِي الْمدينة ، لَم تَزلْ الروح العربيـــة حيةً فيها ، الروحُ الْحافلة بِمصابيحَ من العلم والأدب والفـــن والشـــعر كابن رشد ، وابن زيدون ، والإدريسي ، وابن العوام ، والخلـــف أبي القاسم وابن الخطيب ، وأصحاب الموشحات ...... إن ملكا شيدوه أمسي أثرا من الآثار ، ومجدا أقاموه استحال طللاً من الأطلال ، ومعاهد علـم أسسوها لَم يبقَ منها حجر علي حجر ، وطفتُ كالهائِم الولْهان من برج إلَى متحف إلي قصر ، ووقفت طويلا أمام المئذنة التِي شادها الْمـــهندس العربي جابر للخليفة يوسف بن يعقوب، فانكشفت تَحت عيني مدينة هـي مشرقية بل مغربية في سقوفها البيضاء ، وجادتِها [٢] العوجاء ومصاطبـها الْحافلة بألوان الأزاهيـــر. وحولت نظري إلَى القصر ، وبستانه الفسيح

---

(١) شفقا شفقة وحنانا

(٢) جادتِها : طرقهـــا

الْجميل ، ثُم إلى برج الذهب الذي بناه ابن العلاء علَى ضفتَي النهر الكبير ، فساح بِي الفكرُ وجالت بِي الأحلام ، فأدنتنِي من مَجد العرب الغابر ، بل مثلته أمامي حيا ...... وتساءلت في حيْرة والم ... ما السبب يا ترى فِي سقوط ذلك الملك الذي شعت أنواره فِي ظلمات أوروبا يوماً كنجوم البادية فِي الدجى...؟ ما السبب فِي اضمحلال أركانه وأصوله وقصر عهدهِ وزوال مجده... ؟

وأقول لن أجيب [١] ... فكتب التارخ فيها الكثيْر والعجيب ، ولكني أدعو العرب كل العرب ، ليشاهدوا ما شاهدتُ فِي الأندلس ، ليأخذوا العبرة من الآثار والأطلال ، فيدركوا أسباب سقوطهم ، فيتقوها ، حتّى لا تفجع الأجيال القادمة بأندلس جديدة يضيع مع ضياعها بقايا مَجدنا وبريقُ مستقبلنا.

---

(١) أجيب : الواقع أن الكاتب عالج الأسباب بتوسع لا يصلح له المقام

١٠ - يوميات الطالب

ميخائيل نعيمة

٢٣ آزار ١٩٠٨

عزمتُ ، فِي النهاية، أن أحقِّقَ الفكرةَ التّي أخذتْ تلاحقُنِي وتقلقُنِي من زمان. وهي أن أدوِّن يوميَّاتِي. وإنِّيَّ لأعترِف بأن الذي عجّل فِي تَحقيقها هو أننِي طالعت يوميات "نيكيتين" [١] فكان لَها أعمقُ الأثر في نفسي. حتّى أننِي بقيتُ أسبوعا كاملا بعد مطالعتها لا أفكِّر إلا في أمر واحد ، وهو : لِماذا لا أقتدي بنيكيتين ولو في كتابة اليوميات؟ لعلّنِي ، لو فعلتُ لاكتسبتُ المقدرة على التعبير عن أفكاري بطلاقةٍ وحريَّة ، واكتسبتُ المرونة والسلاسة في الأسلوب.

وهو من كبار الأدباء العرب الذين نقلت كتبهم إلى اللغة الأجنبية، ولد ميخائيل نعيمة سنة ١٨٨٩م بسكنتا (جبل لبنان) درس في فلسطين وروسيا، ثُم درس الحقوق بجامعة واشنطن بالولايات المتحدة. وضع كثيرا من الكتب. تتسم كتاباته بطابع من التأمل الفلسفي في الإنسان والوجود. أديب رفيع يجمع فيه بين عمق التفكير، وروعة التعبير والتصوير، وقد شمل إنتاجاته المقالة والقصة والشعر والنقد فأتحف المكتبة العربية بجواهر قلمه النادرة ودرره الثمينة الغالية.

(١) نيكيتين : شاعر رقيق قد أصدر كتابا بعنوان "يوميات طالب في السمنار"

ما الّذي تتعطّشين إليه يا نفسي، والذي إليه تتوقين؟ أنك تتعطشين إلى مَجد الكاتب وحظُّ الشّاعر... وأيّ الناس لا يطمعُ فِي أن يكون له قلم يتحكم فِي أفكار الناس ، أو يتلاعب بأفئدتِهم إذا ما هو سال بالشعر الرّقراق؟...

٢٤ آزار

.. أمرٌ عجيب! إن الشعر في الأيام الأخيرة يستأثر بكل وعْي ويركّز كلَّ أفكاري علي نقطة واحدة. ومُحاولاتِي الأولَى تبعث الأمل بالنجاح ... وإنّنِي لأعجبُ لِهذا الدَّفق من النشاط الذي أخذت أحسه منذ أن باشرت تدوين يومياتِي. فأنا أقبل على كتابتها إقبال العطشان في القَفر [١] على نبعةٍ من الماء. إنّي أريد أن أكتب وأكتب بغيْر انقطاع ، إلا أنّ التهابا خطيرا في عينِيَّ يكرهني على الإختصار.

... أنْهضُ باكرا. ولكن لا بقصد الإستعداد للدروس التِي بتُّ لا أعيرها كبير اهتمام على نقيض رفاقي الذين لا يفارقُ كتابُ الدرس أيديْهم. كان زمان كان يُهمُّني فيه شرف الأوّليَّة في صفّي. وكان لِي ذلك الشرف فِي الناصرة [٢] وفي سني الأولي هنا ... أما اليوم فإنّي لا أحسد أحدا إلا الذين عيونُهم تُمكنهم من المطالعة حتّى الشبع ... سأفتش عن

(١) القفر : الأرض التِي لا ماء فيها ولا شجر (٢) الناصرة : بلدة فِي فلسطين

مَوضوع للكتابة أستطيع أن أغرق فيه بكلّيتي ، وأن أكرِّس له كل أوقات فراغِي بِحيث لا تضيع منها دقيقة واحدة.

٢٧ آزار

... أفقت صباح اليوم أبكرَ من المعتاد. ومن بعد أن راجعتُ الدرس فِي التاريخ ، خرجت و "اليوشا" لنتنشّق هواء الصباح المنعش .. كان رفيقي يُحدثنِي في أمور جدّيّة ، وكان يتنبأ لِي بالْمجد والشهرة فِي الْمستقبل. وبالطبع ، لن أعيْر تنبُّؤاته اهتماما كبيْرا ...

... تَمر بِي أيام أدخل فيها الصفوف من غيْر أن أكون قد ألقيت حتّى نظرة على الدروس المعيّنة للمذاكرة أن الأحْمرار فِي عينِي يزداد بسبب النور الضئيل الذي يرسله إلينا من السقف قنديل الكاز. لأتوقّف عن الكتابة ، فلغطُ رفاقِي لا يسمح لِي أن أستجمع أفكاري. والأهم من ذلك أن الموضوع الذي بدأت بنظمه لا يترك لِي مَجالا للتفكيْر في أي موضوع غيْره ...

٦ نيسان

... أمس ، وليس لأول مرة، سَمعتُ ملاحظةً من أحد الرقباء بشأن تغيّبِي عن الصلوات في الكنيسة. وقد هدَّد بأن يرفعَ تقريرا بذلك – عنّي وعن ميخائل إسكندر - إلَى الْجمعية الفلسطينية التِي تُنفق على دراستنا.

وذلك أمر قد ينتج عنه تسويد سُمعتنا وسلوكنا ، وحرماننا من الـــدرس. ولو لا ذلك لَما كان حريا بإهتمامنا ... سامح الله إدارتنا، إذا كانت ترى أن حسن السلوك ينحصر في الْمواظبة [١] على الصلوات فِي الكنيســـة فإنّي إرضاء لَها ، سأواظب على الصلوات. ورفيقي الْحمصـــيُّ ، مـــن جانبه، قد وعد أن يواظب مثلِي.

لأدع جانبا مبادئي التِي قلّما أتساهل فيها. فالتَّمسّك بِها فِـــي السـمِنار يعنِي التضحية بالثقافة وبالمستقبل، لست وحدي فِي ما أذهب إليه مـن أن المسيحية الْحقة لا تقوم بالوقوف فِي الكنيسة ساعتين أو ثلاث ســـاعات فِي الآحاد والسبوت والأعياد ، بل باتِّباع تعاليم الإنجيل وإرشاداته ...

١٤ لآذار

فِي المدرسة حركة مَحمومة. إنّها الإمتحانات ... فِي الشـــامن مـــن هـــذا الشهر كان الإمتحان فِي التاريخ. وكان موضوع الْمســـابقة : "أهميـــة الطِّباعة فِي تثقيف الْجماهير الشعبية". وقد أنفقت عليها ساعتين. وبعـــد ثلاثة أيام نقلوا إلَيّ عن لسان أستاذ التاريخ أن مسابقتـــي كانت أفضـــل مسابقة تقدّمت له! .. كل من خبـــر الإمتحانات يعـــرف الإرهـــاق [٢] الذي تسبّبه للطلاب، وكيف أنّها تعطل فيهم كل رغبة فِي أي عمل آخر

---

(١) واظب : الدوام

(٢) الإرهاق : حَمل المرء علي ما لا يطيق

وها أنا لا أحس أي رغبة حتّى في العمل الأحبّ إلَي قلبي. وأعنِي الكتابة ... تسلمت رسالة من الْخال وقبلها بأيام جاءتنِي رسالة من الأخوين فِي "والاّ والاّ [1] " ومعها حوالة بِمئة روبل ، وكنت قد كتبت إليهما أننِي سأمضي الصيف فِي روسيا. إنّهم جَميعهم - الخال والأهل فِي لبنان ، والشقيقين فِي والاّ والاّ - يعقدون علَي آمالا كبيْرة. فأنا - فِي نظر الخال - سأكون ، رجل المستقبل ، و "عِماد الأسرة " و"مَفخرة لبنان" وما أشبه. سأجْمع كل قواي ، أيّها الأعزاء ، وأوجّهها إلي تَحقيق آمالكم. ولكن - هل تُراها تكفي؟ ...

---

(٢) والاّ والاّ : بلد يقع في جنوبي ولاية واشنطن في الولايات المتحدة الأمريكية.

١١ - معنى الإستقلال

عبد الخالق الطريس

الإستقلال ضرورةٌ ، فلذلك نَهتفُ به، ونطلبه، ونستعجلُ الحصول عليه. وإن ثَمن الإستقلال باهظ [(١)] ، ولكنه هيّن يسير فِي نظر جَميع من ذاق مرارة العبودية ، وسئم حياة الذّل ، وفهم معنى الإستقلال ، وخيْرات الإستقلال ، وما يَجنيه من الإستقلال.

معنى الإستقلال — أيّها الْمواطنُ — أن يكون لكَ وطنٌ موفور [(٢)] السيادة، ومقامٌ مَحفوظ فِي حظيرة الدول [(٣)] ، وحكومةٌ منك وأليك تَخدم مصلحتك ، وتتصرف بإرادتك ، وجيش يُحميك فِي السلم و الْحَرب ، وأسطول يَمخر اليم [(٤)] ، ليدفع عنك عوادي النائبات [(٥)] ويَحمل منك

عبد الخالق الطريس هو كاتب من كتاب المملكة المغربية وأحد خطبائِها وموجهيها السياسي. أسهم في الحركات الوطنية قبل الإستقلال وعين بعده سفيْرا للمغرب في أسبانية ثُم فِي جمهورية مصر العربية.

(١) باهظ : ثقيل

(٢) موفور : من وفر المال أي كثره والمقصود هنا : كامل السيادة

(٣) حظيرة الدول : مجتمع الدول ، المجتمع الدولي.

(٤) يُمخر اليم : يشق البحر محدثا صوتا

(٥) النائبات : المصيبة

وإليك ما تَحتاج إلى تصْديره أو توريده ، وأجنحة تطيـرُ ، حاملة اسم بلادك وشعارها [١] لتَربطك بالدنيا!.

معنى الإستقلال - أيّها الْمواطن - أن يَحكم الشّعب نفسه ، ويُشرع لنفسه ، ويصُون حقوقه ومصالحه بنفسه.

معنى الإستقلال - أيّها الْمواطن - ألا يُعرقل لك تطور ، ولا يُفرض عليك اتّجاه غريب ، ولا تُساق فِي الحروب التِي لا مصلحة لك فيها سوق الأنعام [٢] ، ولا تعطل لك قُوة، ولا يُشرع تشريع تكون أنت أول ضحاياه.

معنى الإستقلال أن تكون حقوقُ الإنسان كلها مُحترمةٌ فِي وسطك [٣] ، وأن تكون العدالةُ التِي تُحميك من الإعتداء عدالة نزيْهة منظمة، لا تصل إليها أيدي الْجهال ، ولا يؤثّر فيها أي نفوذ غريب عنها!

معنى الإستقلال أن يُقدّر القدرُ الأدنَى لعيش المواطن ، رجلا كان أو أنثَى حتّى لا يضيع أحد بسبب الفقر أو البطالة أو المرض ، وأن يحصل المواطن على حقه فِي المسكن والْخبز والتعلّم والعلاج ...

---

(١) الشعار : العلامة، الشارة

(٢) الأنعام : البهائم

(٣) الوسط : البيئة وما يحيط بالإنسان

معنى الإستقلال أن ترى فِي بلادك الكفاية من الْمدارس والكليات والْجامعات ومعاهد البحث، والْمكاتب والْمختبرات والْمستشفيات ، والمصحّات والملاجئ والإصلاحيَّات (١) ، والمعامل والمصانع ، وكلها لك ولفائدتك ورفاهيتك!

معنَى الإستقلال أن تكون مُدنك مظهرا رائعا من مظاهر المدنية فِي الْمحافظة علَى الصحة والنظافة وسائر مظاهر التنظيم المدنِي ، وأن تكون قراك قرى صحية نظيفة تَحتوي على كل ما تحتوي عليه القرية فِي الأمم الراقية ، وترتبط فيما بينها بشبكة من المواصلات ، وأن تسير أمور المدينة والقرية بِمجالس منتخبة تسهر على راحة السكان ورفاهيتهم!

معنى الإستقلال أن تنظم أرضك، وتدرس دراسة علمية، وأن يُستغلّ كل شبْر فيها استغلالا فنيا لتنفع فيما تصلح له ، وأن تستغل كل قطرة ماء من مياه أرضك بإنشاء مراكز التوليد الكهربائِي والْخزانات الكافية وتنفيذ مشاريع الرّي(٢) لإحياء الأرض الْموات وتوليد الأرض النَّزور(٣)، وأن يُستخرج ما في بطن الأرض من معادن لتحريك آلة صناعتك،

(١) الإصلاحيات : مكان خاص يدخل إليه المنحرفون من الأولاد بقصد أصلاحهم وتَهذيبهم

(٢) الرّي : إرواء الأراضي الزراعية أو سقيها بطريقة منظمة

(٣) النّزور : الأرض القليلة العطاء

وإيْجاد العمل لأمثالك، وتصنيع كل ما فِي الْميسور من موادها الْخام[١]، ليقلّ الوسطاء ، وتنْزل بذلك الأسعار!

معنى الإستقلال أن يكون لك نظامُ مالي مُحكمٌ ، وأساليب إقتصادية موفَّقة ، وأن يكون لأبناء جلدتك وفر ، وأن يعظم الدخل القومي [٢]، ويرتفع المستوى المعاشي ، وأن تكون نسبة التَّصدير إلَى التوريد نسبة معقولة ، وأن تكون الْميزانية وطنية بكل معانِي الكلمة ، وُضعت للمواطنين ، لصالِحهم ، وصالح بلادهم قبل كل شيء!

الإستقلال وسيلة قبل أن يكون غاية ، فلذلك لا يُمكن أن يُعدُّ حلقة نِهائية فِي سلسلة التطور ، إنه الحلقة الأولَى ، والإصلاح الحقيقي لا يأتِي إلا بعد الإستقلال. ولا خيْر في إصلاح لا يأتِي على يد أبناء البلاد.

---

(١) المواد الخام : المواد الأولية التِي لم تتناولها الصناعة بعد

(٢) الدخل القومي : هو قيمة السلع المنتجة وغيْرها في دولة من الدول في سنة معينة

١٢ - الثقافة العربية بين الشرق والغرب

الأستاذ علي البهلوان

الثقافة كالنهر الجاري ، ينبوعها الحياة ، ومروجها العقل ، مغذيها الْمجتمع، تكون صافيةً نقيةً طالما نبعت من بيئتها ولَم تأخذْ من غيْرها إلا القدر اليسير، وكذلك كانت الثقافةُ العربيةُ فِي الْجاهلية وصدر الإسلام، ثقافة كاملة تغلب عليها البداوة، نفسها قصير قوي، سليمة حيةً، أصولُها ثابتة واضحة ، وميزاتَها بينة جلية ، الطبع قوامها وعمادها وأعظم خصلة فيها ، فقد نبذت الكلفة نبذا، وابتعدت عن التصنع والزخرف. تدفقت الثقافة العربية من عين ثرّة ماؤها صاف غزير، وسرعان ما اتسع النهر المتولد عنها أثر الفتوحات الإسلامية، وأخذت الجداول والأنْهار الكبيرة تصب فيها صبا حاملة معها تراث الشعوب ومدنيات الأمم الغابرة والثقافات السابقة، .. .. والأعجب أن النهر العربي اقتبل تلك الثروات الطائلة من غير أن ينحرف عن مجراه أو يبدل جوهره وطبعه ، بل وهبها من روحه ما امتزجت به وامتزج بِها ، فخرجت الثقافة الكاملة . الثقافة العربية الإسلامية.

وأخذت الثقافات تدخل العربية عن طريق الترجَمة [(١)] ، وعن طريق الشعوب التِي أسلمتْ. وعن طريق التبادل التجاري أيضا ، فنقلوا فلسفة

من مقال للأستاذ علي البهلوان الكاتب التونسي المشهور ـ بتصرف ـ

(١) الترجمة : بدأت حركة الترجمة والإمتزاج بالعناصر الأخرى في العصر العباسي

اليونان وعلومها. وحكمة الْهند وتفكيرها ، وأداب فارس وحضارتِها ، فتراكمت لديْهم الَمعلومات ، وتشعبت المعارف والفنون وتعددت طرق البحث والنتقيب .. واختلطت السبل فِي أول الأمر ، وتعكر ماء النهر الصافي، وصعب هضم ذلك الغذاء لتنوعه وكثرته، ولكن النفس العربية لا تعيش إلا فِي الوضوح ، ولا تزدهر إلا مع البيان ، تغلبت على الغموض فخلّصت الأصول من الفروع المشتبكة ، وأخذ كل علم استقلاله في موضوعه وطريق البحث الصالِحة به ، فتجلى شيئا فشيئا ما بين العلوم من ارتباط وفتحت آفاق جديدة ، وأحدثت علوم لَم تكن، كالجبْر وعلم المجتمع.

وبذلك كانت الثقافة العربية أحسن مثال للثقافة البشرية الكاملة ، لأنّها ثقافة أنسانية يشملها ضرب من الوحدة وأن اتسعت رقعتها ، ولم يكن تنوعها وتشعبها وغزارة موادها وكثرة ابتكاراتِها ، من عوامل التفرقة بينها والتباين بين المثقفين فِي مُختلف أقطارها ، بل زادها كل ذلك غنى وثروة ، وخلق فيها تيارات فكرية ودينية وفنية تربط بين الْمجتمع وتقرب بين الأفراد (١).

---

(١) إشارة إلى اتصال الحركة العلمية والأدبية بين المغرب في الأندلس والشرق في بغداد.

والثقافة العربية في العصر الحديث ، تسعى جاهدةً للتخلص مِما ألصقته بِها القرون من أدران ، وكبلتها [١] به من أشكال وقوالب فارقتها الحياةُ منذ أجيال ، فقد مدت يدها إلَي تراثِها البشري الكبيْر وأخذت تزيح عنه النقاب ، وتنشر كنوزه متعجبة من تراثه ، مكتشفة خفاياه ، مستغربة من التماثل [٢] بينه وبين المدنية الغربية الحاضرة .. ومدَّت اليد الأخرى إلي الثقافة الغربية تكشف عن غناها وجَمالها ، وتغترف من علمها الغزير ومحدثاتِها الْمتجددة ، وعلينا ألا نَخاف من الثقافة ومن الإقبال عليها ، فالثقافة الغربية أو الشرقية ضرورية لنا ، فستكون كاللقاح تُجدد به الأشجار فتأتِي بأطيب الثمرات ، وهي لقاح العقل والذوق ، وأكبَر ميزة لهذه الثقافة اهتمامها بالعلوم الرياضية وتطبيقها وما انتجته من اختراعات تطبيقية قامت عليها نَهضة الغرب والشرق ، فعنايتنا بِها يجب أن تَحتل المكان الأول من تفكيْرنا إذا أردنا الإلتحاق بقافلة الأمم الراقية . وليس في ذلك ما ينافي ثقافتنا ، بل إن ذلك سيعززها ويركزها على أسس ثابتة .. والثقافة لا تعترف بالحدود فهي ملك الإنسانية عامة ، والثقافة تسيْر نَحو الوحدة تُخطي سريعة فقد امتزجت المدنيات ببعضها واقتربت المسافات بينها وأصبح تبادل المعلومات والخبْرات من مُميزات عصرنا الحاضر ..

---

(١) كبلتها : قيدتُها

(٢) التماثل : إشارة إلي أثر العرب فِي الثقافة الغربية

ولقد أصبح من المتفق عليه بين مثقفي الوطن العربي أن الثقافة العربية ليست بعضَ المعلومات اللغوية والبيانية ، بل الثقافة العربية كلّ حيٌّ يشمل تاريْخا يربط أجزاءها ، ومذاهب فلسفية ودينية ، وعلوما تولدت عنها العلوم العصرية، وشعرا ونثرا وعبَرا عن الإنسان في قوالب فنية تُهذّب الذوق والعقل .. فتدريس الثقافة العربية يتطلب جهودا مستمرة لأن البحث العلمي والمتحيص الفكري لم يشملا إلا القليل منها ، فهي مازالت كالبحر الواسع العميق الذي لَم يعرف منه إلا سواحله، فعلينا أن نَخوض غماره [(١)] وأن نصل قدر المستطاع إلى أعماقه ، وعلينا أن نبعد عن ثقافتنا كل ما يُفسد الذوق ويدخل علي العقل الغموض والإعوجاج، ويخرج الإنسان عن طبعه وجبلته ، حتّى نضمن لَها الصلة بالحياة فلا يقترب منها الذبول ، ولا يتسرب إليها الْجمود ويكتنفها التكلف والصنعة , فالثقافة الأصيلة تزيد العقل صقلا ونصوعا والمثقف [(٢)] ليس من يتقن علما من العلوم حتّي يصير مرجعا فيه ، بل العلوم هنا تصبح وسيلة لا غاية، إذ غاية الغايات الإنسان نفسه، الإنسان بعقله وعواطفه وذوقه وإرادته .. فإذا فهمنا ذلك أدركناه أمكننا أن نلعب دورا خالدا في العالم كله ، وأمكننا أن نعيْد لثقافتنا مركزها القوي الثري الذي ضاع بين السلبية والجمود والإتكالية والتخلف.

(١) الغماره : الماء الكثير ومعظم البحر

(٢) المثقف : الإنسان الذي أثر العلم في سلوكه ، أخذ من ثقفت العود أي أزلت ما به من نتوء واعوجاج.

١٣ ــ نحن والماضي

معروف الرصافي
١٨٧٥ - ١٩٤٥

أرى مُستقبل الأيّام الأولى بمطمح [١] يُحاولُ أن يَسُودا [٢]
فَمَا بَلَغَ الْمقَاصِدَ غَيْرُ ساعٍ يُردِّد فِي غَدٍ نَظراً سَدِيْدا [٣]
فَوجّه وجْه عَزْمكَ نَحْو آتٍ وَلا تَلْفتْ إلَى الْمَاضِيْنَ جِيْداً [٤]
وهَلْ إنْ كَان حَاضِرُنَا شَقِيّاً نَسُود بَكونُ مَاضِيْنَا سَعِيداً؟
تقَدّم أَيُّهَا العربيّ شَوْطاً فَإن أمامكَ العَيشُ الرّغِيدا [٥]
وأَسِّس فِي بِنَائِكَ كُلّ مَجْدٍ طَرِيفٍ [٦] واترك الْمجدَ التّلِيداً [٧]

شاعر من شعراء النهضة الأدبية فِي الشرق العربي. هو معروف الرصافي الشاعر العراقي ولد فِي بغداد سنة ١٨٧٥م وحفظ القرآن فِي سن مبكرة، ثُم تتلمذ على العالم اللغوي "إحمد شكري الآلوسي"، وصحبه أثنتي عشرة سنة، يدرس العربية ويُمارس لآدابَها، فوجهه ذلك وجهة أدبية ، وأثر فِي حياته تأثيرا كبيْرا.

إشتهر معروف الرصافي بقصائده الوطنية والإجْتماعية وبِمواقفه الْجرئية التِي لاقى من أجلها الإضطهاد والنفي ويقول بأن للأمة العربية سجل حافل بالأمْجاد وحضارة لا ينكرها الْمنصفون.

(١) المطمح: المطلب ، المقصد
(٢) يُحاول أن يسود: يسعى إلى أن يصبح سيدا
(٣) النظر السدديد: النظر الصائب
(٤) الجيد: العنق، لا تلفت إلي الماضين جيدا: لا تنظر إلَى الْماضي
(٥) العيش الرغيد: العيش النطيب الهنئ
(٦) الطريف: الجديد، ومثله "الطارف"
(٧) التليد: القديْم ومثله :التالد"

فَشَرّ الْعَالَمِيْنَ ذَوو خُمُول إذا فاخَرتَهُمْ ذكروا الجُدودا
وَخَيْرُ النَّاس ذُوحَسَب قَدِيْم أقَام لِنَفْسِهِ حسَبا [١] جَديدا
تَراهُ إذَا ادّعَى فِي النَّاس فَخْراً تُقيمُ له مَكارِمه الشُّهُودا
فَدَعْنِي والفَخَار بأَرض قَوْم مَضَى الزّمنُ القَدِيْم بِهِمْ حَمِيداً
قَد ابْتَسَمَتْ وُجوهُ الدَّهرِ بَيضاً لَهُمْ، ورَأينَنا فَعَبسْنَ سُودا
وقَد عَهدوا لَنَا بتُراث مُلْكٍ أضَعْنَا فِي رِعَايتِهِ الْعُهُودا [٢]
وَعَاشُوا سَادة فِي كُلّ أرضٍ وعِشْنَا فِي مَواطِنِنَا عَبِيْداً
إذَا مَا الْجَهْلُ خَيَّم فِي بِلادٍ رَأيْتَ أَسْوَدهَا مُسخَت قرودا [٣]

---

(١) الحسب: كل ما تعده مفخرة ومَجدا

(٢) العهود: المواثيق جَمع "عهد"

(٣) مسخت: أبدلت وتَحولت

١٤ ــ إلى المجْهول

عبد الرحمن شكري
١٨٨٦ - ١٩٥٨

يَحوطني مِنْكَ بَحر لست أعرفَــهُ ومَهمَه لستُ أدري ما أقــاصيه [١]
أقضِي حَياتِي بنفس لست أعرفهَا وحَولِي الْكون لَم تُدرك مَجاليه [٢]
ياليت لِي نظرة للغيب تُسعــدنِي لعــل فيه ضيــاء الحــق يُبــديه
وليت لِي خطوة تدحو مَجــاهلــه وتكشف الستر عن خافي مساعيه [٣]
كأن روحِي عــود أنت تُحكــمه فابسط يديــك واطلق من أغانيــه

ولد عبد الرحْمن شكري ببور سعيد (مصر) سنة ١٨٨٦م وبعد تكميل دراســته الثانوية التحق بِمدرسة المعلمين العليا وتَخرج فيها سنة ١٠٩٠م وقد التــزم فيــها الدرس الصارم للأدبين العربِي والغربِي.

توضيح: أول ما يلاحظ علي هذه القصيدة أن موضوعها جديد، فالقصيدة القديْمة لَم تكن تتحدث عن الْمجهول إنّما كانت تتحدث دائِما عن الْمعلوم، عن مديــح شخص أو رثائه أو هجائه، ولَم تتعلق بِما وراء ذلك إلا نادرا وفِي حكم جزئية. أما هنا فَمشكلة الْمجهول تثار فِي دائرة واسعة، وتظهر حيْرة الشاعر وقلق عقلــه إزاء الكون وأسرار الْحياة.

الشاعر يُخاطب الْمجهول فالْحياة جَميعها ــ أمام عينيه ــ مَجامل وألغاز ويتمــنى لو استطاع أن يطلع على هذه الْمجامل والألغاز. وهو يريد أن يعرف حقائق الحياة حتّى يصورها بقلمه في قرطاسه أو يلحنها على نايه.

(١) الْمهمه : المفــازة (٢) مَجاليه: مناظره ومشاهده

(٣) تدحو : تبسط

وأكبَر الظــن أنّي هــالك أبــداً شوقــا إليك وقلبي فيــه ما فِيــه
من حسرَة وإبــاء لست أملكــه يــأبَى لِي العيش لَم تُدرك معانيــه
وأنت فِي الكون من قاض ومقترب قــد استوى فيك قــاصيه ودانيه
كأنّي منك فِــي نــاب لِمفتــرس الــمرء يسعى ولغز العيش يُدميــه
كَم تَجعل العقل طفلا حار حــائره وربّ مطلب قــد خاب باغيــه
فــأنت كالليل والأفهــام حــائرة مثل العيون علاها منك داجيــه[٢]
ليل مهيب كلجّ البحــر حندسُــهٌ تكاد تسمع منــه صوت طاميه[٣]
فليتــهُنّ خفافــيش بلــوح لَهَــا مَجاهل الــحق خافــيه وباديــه
بل لَيت لِي فِكرة كالكون واسعة أدحو بِها الكــون تبدو لِي خوافيه
ليس الطمُوح إلَى المجهول من سفه ولا السمو إلَــى حــقّ بِمكــروه
إن لَم أنل منه ما أروى الغليل[٤] به قــد يَحمد المرء ماء ليس يرويــه
يــا قلب يهنيك نبضٌ كله حرقٌ إلَى الغرائب مِما غــزّ ســاميــه

تسيطر على أفكار الشاعر نزعة عقلية واضحة، وكأنه يريد للشــعر وألفاظــه أن تكون أوعية للعقل قبل أن تكون أوعية للخيال، وهو لذلك لا يعمد إلي تشــبيهات واستعارات كثيْرة على طريقة القدماء، فهو يُخاطب العقل، والعقــل لا يــهتم إلا بالحقائق.

(١) داجيــة: مظلمة وخفيــة (٢) الحندس: الظلام، طامية: مرتفعة

(٣) الغليل: حرارة الشمس

فالعيش حبّ لِما استعصت مسالكه تَجـارب الْمرء تُدميـه وتُعليـه
كَم ليلـة بتّما ولـهان ذا أمـل لَم يسل قلبِي أن غابت أمـانيـهِ
لعل خاطر فكر طارقِـي عرضـا يَـدنو بِما أنا طول العُمر أبغِيـهِ
يوضح الغامض المستور عن فطن وأفهم العَيش تستـهوي بَواديـه
هيهات ما كشفت لِي الحق خاطرة ولَم يُجب لِـي سوالا ما أناديـه

١٥ ــ لا أريد

خالد محمد الفرج

لا أريد الْمال أكداسا، لَجينا[١] أو نضارْ
فِي "بُنوك" عامرات، أو خزانات كبارْ
أو قصورا شامِخات، أو نَخيلا أو عقارْ
أو رفاها من نعِيم العيش ما شاء اليَسار[٢]

وأنا أنظر حولِي ، كم عليهَا من فَقِير

لا أريد السعد أن يدخل بيتِي بالهناء
لست يا هذا سعيدا وأرى حولِي الشقاء
صحتي سقم إذ الْمرضى يعانون البلاء
غَير أنّي باسم للموت إن جاء الفناء

كُل من أنظر حولِي إلي الموت يصير

خالد مُحمد الفرج من شعراء الكويت القدامى وكان من أصدقاء الشاعر صقر الشبيب ومن معاصريه

(١) اللجين : الفضة ، النضار : الذهب (٢) اليسار : الغنى

لا أريـــد الشمس تسبيِني [١] بانـــوار الشروق
أنـــا لا أنظـــر للروض بـــالحاظ [٢] الشفـــوق
غـــادتـــي لا تحسبِي صدى جفاء أو عقـــوق [٣]
كل حســـن أو بَهـــاء أو جَمـــال لا يـــروق

وأنـــا أنظر حـــولِي ، كـــم عليهَـــا من ضريـــــر

أيّـــهـــا البـــلبل مهـــلا لاتغـــرد فِـــي الغصن
قطع الأوتار يـــا عـــازف، واهدأ فِي سكون
لا أريـــد الاذن أن تسمع نغـــما أو شجـــون
لا صريرا، لا عزيفـــا، لا رنينـــا، لا حنيـــن

أنـــا أنظر حولِـــي، الصم فـــي الدنيـــا كثْيـــر

---

(١) تسبيـــنـــي : تـــاسرنـــي
(٢) اللحـــظ : بـــاطن العيـــن ـــ جزمعة لحـــاظ والحاظ
(٣) عقوق : العصيان وعـــدم الشفقة

١٦ ـ فلسفة الحيـــاة

إيلياء أبو ماضي
١٨٨٩ - ١٩٥٧

أيهـــذا الشـــاكي ومـــا بك داء كيف تغـــدو إذا غدوت عليلا[١]
إن شـــر الجناة فـــي الأرض نفس تتـــوفى قبل الرحيل الـــرحيـــلا
وترى الشوك في الورود وتعمـــي أن تـــرى فوقها النـــدى إكليلا[٢]
والـــذي نفـــسه بغيـــر جمـــال لا يـــرى في الوجود شيئا جميلا

أبو ماضي من كبار شعراء المهجر ولد في لبنان سنة ١٨٨٩م وهاجر إلى مصر ثـم إلى أمريكا سنة ١٩١٢م ومكث أربع سنوات لا يقول شعرا ولعله كان مشـــغولا بتوبير عيشه وانضم إلى الرابطة القلمية بنيويورك حيـــن تأسيسها سنة ١٩٢٠م.

وقد أتاحت له هجرته إلى أمركا التزود من ينابيع الثقافة الغربية وقوى اتصاله بها أنه كان من المشتغلين بالصحافة وعضوا بارزا في "الرابطة القلمية" غير أنه لم ينس الأدب العربي القديم بل ظل يداوم الإطلاع عليه. فكان من هذا المزيج شخصية شعرية جديدة.

توضيح: تدور القصيدة حول فكرة واحدة هي أن الإحساس بالجمال في الوجـــود يستلزم نفسا جميلة تحعس به، وقد دعا أبو ماضي كل شخص أن يستشـــعر هـــذه النفس ليحس الغبطة في الحياة. فالقصيدة موحدة الفكر وهو توحيد يجر وحـــدة فنية واضحة في بنائها وتعاقب أبياتها.

---

(١) الغدو: الرجوع وقت الغداة، ضد الرواح (٢) الإكليل: التاج والعصابة تزين بالجواهر

فتـــمتّـــع بالصبـــح مادمت فيـــه لا تَخف أن يزول حتّـــى يـــزولا
أدركت كنهَهـــا[١] طيور الرّوابِي فمِن العـــار أن تظـــل جَهـــولا
تتغنّـــى والصقر قـــد ملك الْجـــوّ عليهَـــا والصائدون السبيـــلا
تغنّي وعُمرهـــا بعـــض عـــام أفـــتبكي وقـــد تعـــيش طويـــلا
فاطلب اللهو مثلها تطلب الأطـــيار عند الْهجير [٢] ظلاًّ ظليـــلاً
وتعـــلم حـــبّ الطبيـــعة منهـــا واتْـــرك القال للورى والقيـــلا[٣]
أنـــت لـــلأرض أولا و أخيـــرا كنت ملكا أو كنت عبدا ذليـــلا
كُل نَجـــم إلَى الأفـــول ولكـــن آفة النّجم أن يَخـــاف الأفـــولا[٤]
فإذا ما وجدت فِي الأرض ظـــلا فتـــفيأ[٥] به إلَى أن يَحـــولا[٦]
وتـــوقع إذا السماء اكفـــهرت[٧] مطرا فِي السهول يُحي السهـــولا

القصيدة بِهذه الصورة تفتح آفاقا واسعة أمام القارئ، إذ تَجعله يفكر فِي الإنســـان والحياة والكن وتفسح له فِي التخيل والوهم. وهِي ناحية مهمة فِي الشعر الحديث، إذ ينطلق فيه الفكر إلي آماد واسعة، ولا ريب فِي أن مصدر ذلك اتســـاع ثقافـــة الشاعر من ناحية وصدق وشعوره وإحساسه المباشر بدنياه وما فيـــها مـــن متعـــة وجَمال.

(١) كنهها : حقيقتها (٢) الهجير : نصف الهار عند اشتداد الحر
(٣) القال والقيل : الكلام الطيب والخبيث (٤) الأفول : الغروب
(٥) تفيأ : استظل يـــحول : يتحول
(٦) وبيـــل : وخيـــم (٧) الكبل : القيـــد

ما اتينا إلَى الحياة لنشقى فأريْحوا أهل العقول العقولا
كل من يَجمع الهموم عليه أخذتْه الْهموم أخذاً وبيلا[١]
كن هزارا فِي عشه يتغنّى ومع الكبل[٢] لايبالي الكبولا
لا غرابا يطارد الدود فِي الأر ض ويوما فِي الليل يبكي الطلولا
كن غديرا يسيْر فِي الأرض رقرا قا[٣] فيسقي عن جانبيه الْحقُولا
لا وعاء يقيد الْماء حتَى تستحيل الْمياه فيه وحولا
كن مع الفجر نسمة توسع الأز هار شَمًّا وتارة تقبيلا
لاسِموما[٤] من السوافي [٥] اللواتِي تَملأ الأرض فِي الظلام عويلا
ومع الليل كوكبا يُؤنس الغا بات والنّهر والربَى والسهولا
لا دحي يكره العوالِم والنا س فيلقي على الْجميع سدولا[٦]
أيُّهذا الشاكي وما بك داء كُن جَميلا ترى الوجود جَميلا

---

(١) وبيل : وخيم (٢) الكبل : القيد
(٣) رقراقا : متلألئا (٤) السموم : القيد
(٥) السوافي : الرياح المحملة بالتراب (٦) السدول : الأستار

١٧ ـ نشيد أفريقيـــة

محمد الفيتوري

يا أخي في الشرق في كل سكـــن يا أخي في الأرض في كل وطـــن
أنـــا أدعـــوك فهـــل تعرفنـــي يـــا أخـــا أعرفه رغـــم المحن[١]
إنـــي مزقت أكفـــان الدجـــى إنـــي هـــدمت جدران الوهن[٢]
لم أعد مقبرة تـــحكي البلـــى[٣] لم أعـــد ساقيـــة تبكي الدمن[٤]
أنـــا حـــي خـــالد رغم الـــردى أنـــا حـــر رغـــم قضبان الزمـــن
إن نكن سرنا على الشوك سنينـــا ولقينـــا من أذاه مـــا لقـــينـــا
إن نكـــن بتـــنا عراة جائـــعينـــا أو نكـــن عشنـــا حفاة بائسينـــا
إن نكن أوهنت[٥] الفـــأس قوانـــا فوقفنـــا نتـــحدى الظـــالمينـــا[٦]
إن نكـــن سخرنـــا جـــلادنـــا فبنينـــا لأمـــانينـــا سجـــونـــا[٧]
لقـــد ثرنـــا علـــى أنفسنـــا[٧] ومحـــونا وصمـــة الـــذلة فينـــا

محمد الفيتوري شاعر سوداني معاصر. ولد سنة ١٩٣٠م من أب ســـوداني وأم مصرية. انهى تعلمه في القاهرة. تميز شعر محمد الفيتوري بـــالدفق والعـــاطفي والحمية الثورية. وهـــا هو هنا يدعو إلى تحطيم القيود وتحرر أفريقية من العبودية والخضوع.

(١) المحن : البلايا والمصائب، المفرد محنة
(٢) الدجى : الظلام، الوهن: الضعف
(٣) البلـــى : القدم
(٤) الدمن : جمع دمنة، وهي آثار الديـــار
(٥) أوهنت : أضعفت
(٦) نتحدى الظالم : ننازعه لنغلبـــه
(٧) بنينا لأمانينا سجونا: أخفينا لما ينزل بنـــا من عذاب
(٨) ثرنا على أنفسنا : حملنا علي إظهار الأماني

الْملايين أفاقت من كراها[١] ما تراها ملأ الأفق صداها ؟
خرجَتْ تَبحث عن تاريْخها بعد أن تاهت علَى الأرض وتاها[٢]
حَملت أفؤسَها وانْحدرت من روابِيها وأغوار قراها[٣]
فانظر الإسرار فِي أعينِها وصباح البعث بَيحتاج الْجباها[٤]
يا أخِي في كل أرض وجِمت [٥] شفتاها واكفهرت[٦] مقلتاها
قُم تُحرر من توابيت الأسى لست أعْجوبتها أو مومياها[٧]
إنطلق فوق ضحاها ومساها يا أخِي قد أصبح الشعب إلّها[٨]

---

(١) الكري : النوم

(٢)خرجت تَبحث عن تاريخها: تبعد مجدها أو تنشئ لَها مجدا يسطره التاريخ

(٣) الأغوار : جمع غور وهو المكان المنخفض

(٤) يَحتاج الجباة :يظهر على الجباه والوجوه

(٥) وجمت : اشتد حزنها و أسكتها عن الكلام

(٦) اكفهرت مقلتاها : المراد ظهر الحزن فِي عينيها

(٧) مومياها : الجسد المحنط، على الطريقة التي اتبعها قدماء المصريين في تحنيط أجساد ملوكهم وعظمائهم.

(٨) أصبح الشعب إلها : أي أنه أصبح يَملك قدره وكأنه إله.

١٨ ـ أخـي الإنسان

عيسى النـاعوري

أخـي فـي العـالَم الـواسـع فِـي الـمـغرب والـمَـشرق
أخِـي الأبيـض والأسـود فِـي جـوهـرك الْمُطـلـق[١]
أمـدّ يـدي ، فصـافحـهـا تَجد قلبِـي بِهـا يـخفـق

بُـحبـك يـا أخِـي الإنسـان

أحـبـك دون مـا نـظَـر إلـي لـونـك أو جِـنـسك
وأكـره مـن يَبُـث الْحقـد[٢] فِـي نَفسي وفِـي نفسِـك
لتـرقـص أنت فِـي بُـؤسـي وكَـي أرقـص فِـي بـؤسك

ونشْقَـى يـا أخِـي الإنسـان

أخِـي مـأسـاتـنا ليسـت سِـوى مـن صنـع أيـدينـا
فَمَـن اطـمـاعنا الشعـواء[٣] سـوّدنـا لـيـالـيـنـا
ومن أحـقـادنـا الـعميـاء هـدّمـنـا أمـانـيـنـا

فـرفقـا يـا أخِـي الإنسـان

حيـاته: ولد عيسى الناعوري فِي الأردن سنة ١٩١٨م هو كاتب أردنِي اشـتغل بالتـدريس وأنتج عـدة آثار في دراسة الأدب ونقده وبِخاصة المهجري منه.

(١) جوهرك المطلق : طبيعتك غير المقيد:ة بشيء (٢) يبث : ينشر

(٣) الشعواء: : الشـديدة

لــقـــد جئـنـــا إلــى الدنيـــا مـــعـــا لــنـعيش إخـــوانـــا
ونـــســـعـــد بـــالــحيـــاة معـــا أحـــبّــــاء وأعـــوانـــــا
ولو شئـنـــا أحلــنـــا[٢] جـنــــ ـــــة الفـــردوس دُنــيـــانـــا

فـــهيّـــأ يـــا أخِـــي الإنســـان

تـــعـــال نـــقم حـــضـــارات مـــعـــا، ولـــنـــرفـــع العمـــران
ونـــخلـــق فِـــي الـــحيـــاة لنـــا مـــبـــاهـــج حلـــوة الألـــوان
وضـــع يُـــمنـــاك فِي يـــمنـــأي فِـــي دعـــة[٣] وفـــي إطمعنـــان

لـــنسعـــد يـــا أخِـــي الإنســـان

دع الأطـــمـــاع والأحـــقـــاد لا تَـــتجـــعـــل لَـــهـــا شـــأنـــا
فلـــن تســـعـــد بـــالأطـــمـــاع أو تـــرفـــع بُـــنْـــيـــانـــا
ولـــن تَـــمنـــحـــك الأحـــقـــاد فـــي دُنْـــيـــاك سُلـــطـــانـــا
فـــدعـــهـــا يـــا أخِـــي الإنســـان

القصيدة من الشعر الإنساني يدعو الشاعر فيها إلَى السحب والرفق والسعادة رغما عن إختلاف الألسنة والألوان والجنسيات وبالتعاون البشري وتزدهر ألإنسانية.

(١) أحلنـــا : جـعلنـــا

(٢) فِـــي دعـــة : فـــي سكينـــة

تُــثيــر الْــحرب ؟ قل لِي هــل ســتــنْجــو أنت فِي الْــحرب؟
ألا يُــشــقِيــك أن أفْــنَــى بِــنــارك دُون مــــا ذنْــب ؟
وهــلْ يَــرتــاح إذْ تَــفْــنَــى ضَــمِيْــري الْــحــرّ أو قَلْبِــي؟

رويـــدا يــا أخِــي الإنســان

فــبيتــك يــا أخِــي بَــيــتِــي ودربُك فِــي الــدُّنْيــا دربِــي
وعِــزُّك لَــهــو مِــن عــزي وحُبُّــك يَــا أخِــــي حُــبِّــي
ومــا تَلــقــاه مــن ضَــيــم تُــصِيــبُ سَــهــامُــه قَلْبِــي

فــيدمــي يــا أخِــي الإنســان

كــلانــا نَــعــرف الأشــواق والآمــال تَــحـــدونــا[٦]
كــلانــا نشتــهــي والْحســن لا يَــنْــفــك يُــغْــريــنــا
كــلانــا نــعــرف الأســرا ر نَــبــلوهــا وتَــبْــلونــا[٧]

فــمــهلا يــا أخِــي الإنســان

أخِــي! نَــحن التــقينــا اليــو م فِــي الــدنيــا بــلا مــوعــد
ودرب الْــعــمــر مثــل الْحلــم مــهمــا طــال لــن يَــخلــد
سَــنْمضِي مثــلمــا جــئــنــا وذاك مــصيــرنــا الأوحـــد

ســلامــا يــا أخِــي الإنســان

---

(١) تَحدونــا : تســوقــنــا
(٢) تــبلونــا : تــجــربنــا

١٩ ــ وجـود جديد

إلياس قنصل

مـــا ترانِـــي أجيل فـــي الأفـــق أنظـــاري وحيدا أخاطب المجهولا؟
أن تسلنـــي ماذا أريد فما تسمـــع مـــن ردى مطلـــبا مـــعقـــولا
حولِي الناس يَمرحـــون اكتفـــاء ويبـــاهـــون بالقضـــاء قبـــولا
وأنـــا واجـــم كـــأنّـــي فـــي قفـــر بعيـــد وقد أضعت الـــدليلا
أتَـــمنـــى لـــو كـــنت لا شيء أو كان وجـــودي عن أي شيء بديلا
أيـــن لِي دفقة من الْحق والعرفان تَجلـــو أمام عقلـــي السبيـــلا ؟
أنا فِي قبضـــة الْعـــذاب رهيـــن أثقلتـــنـــي خواطـــري تكبيـــلا
لا تُحـــاول تَخفيف عبئـــي فلـــن تلقـــي لأسبـــاب حيـــرتِي تعليلا
أتلهـــى بِما يوسوس لِـــي الفـــن فألقـــي على اكتئابـــي ســـدولا
أن تنـــل كفـــى ما يعـــز منـــالا لَم تَجـــده عينـــأي الا ضئيـــلا
لست أخشـــى السنين تزرع دربي نكبـــات تسك نفســـي عويـــلا

إلياس قنصل ولد فِي يبرود فـــي سوريـــا (١٩١١م) وانتقـــل بـــه والـــده إلى الأرجنتين. وقـــد أقام إلياس في ديار الهجرة إلَى عام ١٩٥٥م لكن لَم يَجد الأمور فيه كما كان يتخيلها ويرجوها إذا عـــاد إلَى الأرجنتين عام ١٩٥٨م . وموهبتـــه الأدبية متنوعة الْمجالات فهو ينظم الشعر ويكتب الأقصوصة ويَخوض فِي النقـــد الأدبِي وفِي الْمعالجات الإجْتماعية والسياسية وهو يَميل فِي كتاباته النثرية.

انّما أرهب الفراغ الذي ألْمسه حولي بكرة وأصيلا
وأمل الزهور تبدو حسانا ثُم تنأى عن الْجمال ذبولا
وأعاف الكلام يتلى بيانا ثُم يَخفى كأنه ما قيلا
أفهمتني الْحياة أنّي غبي حين أدعو سرابَها سلسبيلا
هذه الدنيا مسرح فاض هزلا أنا فيه لا أحسن التمثيلا
كل ما ضمه الزمان هباء شأنه أن يزول أو أن يَحولا
والْخلود الذي أكد إليه أن أفسره بشبه التضليلا
عبثا أرتَجي بلوغ الأمانِي وأمانِي تنشد المستحيلا
أشتهي أن ارى وجودا جديدا ليس هذا الوجود يروي الغليلا

٢٠ ـ القمر العاشق

مهداة إلى الشاعر القصصي الكبير الأستاذ إبراهيم العريض

الأستاذ أحمد محمد آل خليفة

تقــول سعاد فِي جيــان لأمّهـــا هل البدر - يا أماه - في الليل يعشق؟
فهشّت وقــالت فِي دلال ورقّــة وكانت لإحساس الصبية تشفق ؟
يقــولون: كانت فِي القديْم صبية تضيء بآفاق الْجمــال وتشــرق
تطــل من الشبــاك كل عيشــة وفِي وجهها من معدن الحسن رونق!
فلمــا رآها البدر فِي الليل راعية جَمال صباها وهْو بالسحر ينطــق
فهمّ يزور الأرض من أجل حسنها ويعصي لظي للجاذبيــة يصعــق
تــراءى وأومي من بعيــد بقلبــه إليهــا وفِي عينيــه شوق معتّــق
وقال : ألا هل تقبليــن زيارتِــي فــإني إلَى خــدر الْهوى أتشوّق
ســاهبط فِي رفق إليــك لأنَّــنِي لِمرآك - من بعد - أعص وأشرق!
وبِي منك أشواق ولا قلب فِي الورى يُحس بِها، حيث الْمحبة تَحــرق
وحاول خلع الــجاذبية فانبــرى لَهيب يدوّي فِي السّماء ويبــرق
وغطي اللهيب الأرض واحتدم اللظى أوشك - يوم الحشر - بالخلق يطبق
وما العشق الا ثورة النفس فِي الورى تَحل لِمن فِي الحب بالوعد يصدق!!

الأستاذ أحمد محمد آل خليفة من البرحين

٢١ ـ أغنية الساقية

الدكتور أحمد محمد المعتوق

بُــعِيد ما تنضَج تفاحة غاباتنا
ويتضُجُ النبق ، وتُبرز الكنوزُ ما حوتْه من درر
ويَهتف الرب : أيا ذا الْجنــاح
كُن ، فيكــون الصبــاح
ويسكر الضوء علَى دالية الفجر ويندي الوتــر
بُــعِيد ما تنضَج تفاحة غاباتنا
وتقــرع الباب تعيد الصبــاح
ترتِيلة الساقية
وتسحب الذّيل علَى الرابيةْ
تزلَق الضوء علَى الآنية
يَهتِف : يا فاتنة النهار يامعين شَمسه
حَواء يا أغنية الساقية
قد ملأَ الدورقَ همس المطر
وانسرح الظلّ كنهر مباح

الدكتور أحمد مُحمد المعتوق شاعر وأستاذ جامعي وكاتب من الْمملكة العربيــــة السعودية

يركُضُ في ضاحية العُمر فتخضرّ رفاة البشر
ويطْعم الخلق نَضيج الثمر
ويغمِس الطائر منقاره
فِي شفق الشمس فلا يستعِر
قد تعِب الشوق فيـــا من ظفر !
سَمعتُها أغنية الساقية
فِي ليلة أنْجمها راقدة ، فِي ليلق شاتية
سَمعتها وحيـــرة الغريب فِي حروفِها
ولَحنها كأنه الجريح كالرنين فِي الضلوع
بليلة ساهرة غافية
كِلاُبها السود عدت جائعة لاهثة عاوية
تَحوم حول الرابية
سَمعتها حواء فِي ليلتها العارية
تنشج والرياح خلف بابِها تأزٌّ والدوار
يضج فِي ستائر الأصيل
فِي الغرفة الحمراء والرفوف والمرايا
فِي الشال فِي طنافس الحرير فِي حقائب الرحيل
وهمسها ، وزفرة توقدها عند جبال الضجر :
يالرغيف بارد يأكله السهر!

وقُبلة أرخص من قهقهة الريح بِمهوى الحجر!
وعندما ينقر مرآتِها
تفرح أم تفزع أم تَمنعه أن يطيْر !!
تَهمس : يا فرخ رماك المساء
وبعدما شبّ جناحاك رماك المساء
فِي وحل الدرب كسير الجناح
يَمضغ منقارك شوك الطريق
يشرب نَهر العقيق
ويضرم النار بجفنيك فيا للحريق!!
وصفت من أجنحة الزنبق للصدر وشاح
وقلت لِي : قد ملأ الدورق همس المطر
وانسرح الظل كما الخيمة فِ حضنِها يُقمر لون السمر
بنيت لِي العرش وقلت احملي
فوق ذراعيك جنون الهوى
ورقصي تَحت ندى الفجر قلوب البشر
أسقط كالنيزك ذاك الملاك
في سدم الوحشة كالصرخة أو كالْهباء
وراح غول الليل ما أوحشه
يسلخ وجه القمر

يسرق ظلّ الشجر

وجنة قد عرشت للنجم حلو كرمها

ولألأت للطير ضوء حلمها

فِي الليلة الماضية

يتقد الصيف على جفونِها

ويسهر الغراب فوق دوحها

صوحت الواحة ، والساقية

تركتها يابسة القلب علي المنحدر!

Arabic Language and Middle Eastern Interest Titles from Hippocrene Books

HISTORY & CULTURE

The Middle Eastern Kitchen
240 pages • 8 x 10½ • color photographs • ISBN 0-7818-1023-X • NA • $29.95hc • 487

The Arab World: An Illustrated History
312 pages • 5½ x 8½ • ISBN 0-7818-0990-8 • W • $14.95pb • 465

A History of the Islamic World
224 pages • 5½ x 8½ • ISBN 0-7818-1015-9 • W • $22.50hc • 545

Treasury of Arabic Love: Poems, Quotations and Proverbs in Arabic and English
128 pages • 5 x 7 • ISBN 7818-0395-0 • W • $11.95hc • 71

Women in Islam: An Anthology from the Qu'ran and Hadiths
Expanded Second Edition
256 pages • 5½ x 8½ • ISBN 0-7818-1090-6 • NA • $18.95pb • 9

Saudi Arabia: From Bedouin Beginnings to Modern Kingdom
Expanded Edition
376 pages • 5 x 8 • ISBN 0-7818-1097-3 • NA • $14.95pb • 117

Voices of American Muslims
300 pages • 5½ x 8½ • ISBN 0-7818-1054-X • W • $22.50hc • 52

Egypt: An Illustrated History
160 pages • 5 x 7 • ISBN 0-7818-0911-8 • W • $12.95pb • 311

LANGUAGE INSTRUCTION GUIDES

Mastering Arabic with 2 Audio CDs
320 pages • 6 x 9 • ISBN 0-7818-1042-6 • NA • $29.95pb • 66

Pocket Guide to Arabic Script
104 pages • 4 x 6 • ISBN 0-7818-1104-X • W • $6.95pb • 209

Beginner's Iraqi Arabic with 2 Audio CDs
250 pages • 5 1/2 x 8 1/2 • ISBN 0-7818-1098-1 • W • $29.95pb • 034

Arabic Grammar of the Written Language
550 pages • 5½ x 8½ • ISBN 0-87052-101-2 • W • $22.50pb • 397

Basic Arabic Workbook
352 pages • 8½ x 11 • ISBN 0-7818-1126-0 • NA • $29.95pb • 288

PHRASEBOOKS & DICTIONARIES

Emergency Arabic Phrasebook
80 pages • 7½ x 4½ • ISBN 0-7818-0976-2 • NA • $5.95 • 467

Arabic-English/English-Arabic Compact Dictionary
3,800 entries • 200 pages • 3⅛ x 4⅝ • 0-7818-1044-2 • W • $8.95pb • 651

Arabic-English/English-Arabic Practical Dictionary
18,000 entries • 440 pages • 4⅜ x 7 • 0-7818-1045-0 • NA • $22.50pb • 632

Arabic-English/English-Arabic Standard Dictionary
30,000 entries • 460 pages • 5½ x 8½ • 0-7818-0383-7 • W • $24.95pb • 195

Arabic-English/English-Arabic Concise Dictionary, *Romanized*
Egyptian and Syrian Dialect
4,500 entries • 325 pages • 4 x 6 • ISBN 0-7818-0686-0 • W • $12.95pb • 775

Arabic-English/English-Arabic Dictionary and Phrasebook
4,500 entries • 220 pages • 3¾ x 7½ • ISBN 0-7818-0973-8 • W • $12.95 • 445

Hippocrene Children's Illustrated Arabic Dictionary
500 entries • 94 pages • 8½ x 11 • ISBN 0-7818-0891-X • W • $11.95pb • 212

Modern Military Arabic Dictionary
English-Arabic/Arabic-English
204 pages • 5½ x 8½ • ISBN 0-7818-0841-3 • W • $13.95 • 229

OTHER TITLES OF REGIONAL INTEREST

Dari-English/English-Dari Dictionary and Phrasebook
5,000 entries • 232 pages • 3¾ x 7 • ISBN 0-7818-0971-1 • W • $11.95pb • 443

Beginner's Dari With Audio CD
178 pages • 5½ x 8½ • ISBN 0-7818-1139-2 • W • $19.95pb • 275

Farsi-English/English-Farsi Dictionary and Phrasebook
4,000 entries • 240 pages • 3¾ x 7½ • ISBN 0-7818-1073-6 • W • $11.95pb • 398

Farsi-English/English-Farsi Concise Dictionary
8,400 entries • 420 pages • 4 x 6 • ISBN 0-7818-0860-X • W • $1495pb • 260

Pashto-English/English-Pashto Dictionary and Phrasebook
5,000 entries • 232 pages • 3¾ x 7½ • ISBN 0-7818-0972-X • W • $11.95pb • 429

Introduction to Pushtu, ***Romanized***
350 pages • 5¼ x 8½ • ISBN 0-7818-0939-8 • W • $14.95pb • 369

Beginner's Persian
292 pages • 5½ x 8½ • ISBN 0-7818-0567-8 • W • $14.95pb • 696

Tajik-English/English-Tajik Concise Dictionary
8,000 entries • 200 pages • 4 x 6 • ISBN 0-7818-1118-X • W • $11.95pb • 246

Tajik-English/English -Tajik Dictionary and Phrasebook
1,400 entries • 176 pages • 3¾ x 7½ • ISBN 0-7818-0662-3 • W • $11.95pb • 752

Turkmen-English/English-Turkmen Dictionary and Phrasebook
4,000 entries • 232 pages • 3¾ x 7½ • ISBN 0-7818-1072-8 • W • $11.95pb • 497

Urdu-English/English-Urdu Dictionary and Phrasebook
4,000 entries • 176 pages • 3¾ x 7½ • ISBN 0-7818-0970-3 • W • $11.95pb • 427

Prices subject to change without notice. **To purchase Hippocrene Books,** contact your local bookstore, call (718) 454-2366, or write to: HIPPOCRENE BOOKS, 171 Madison Avenue, New York, NY 10016. Please enclose check or money order, adding $5.00 shipping (UPS) for the first book, and $.50 for each additional book.